The Theatre Student

LEARNING SCENES/BASIC ACTING

ARISTOPHANES TO ALBEE

The Theatre Student

LEARNING SCENES /
BASIC ACTING

ARISTOPHANES TO ALBEE

Gerald Lee Ratliff

PUBLISHED BY
RICHARDS ROSEN PRESS, INC.

NEW YORK, N.Y. 10010

Published in 1981 by Richards Rosen Press, Inc.
29 East 21st Street, New York, N.Y. 10010

Copyright 1981 by Gerald Lee Ratliff

First Edition

Library of Congress Cataloging in Publication Data

Ratliff, Gerald Lee.
    Learning scenes/basic acting.

    (The Theatre student)
    SUMMARY: Includes scenes from period, modern, and
avant-garde plays with instructions on how to prepare
for and play each scene.
    1. Acting. 2. Drama—Collections. [1. Acting]
I. Title.
PN2080.R37   792'.028   80–18029
ISBN 0–8239–0531–4

Manufactured in the United States of America

ABOUT THE AUTHOR

GERALD LEE RATLIFF is Assistant Professor, Theatre, as well as Deputy Chairman and Graduate Advisor, at Montclair State College, Upper Montclair, New Jersey. Among other professional activities, he is president of the Speech and Theatre Association of New Jersey, editor of the national theatre journal *The Cue,* and associate editor of *Communication Quarterly.* He is also U.S.A. poetry editor of *Inscape* (Harlow, England) and a fellow of the International Academy of Poets.

Mr. Ratliff is the author of numerous papers and articles for periodicals, among them "Manners and Movement: Performance and Production Perspectives on Playing Period Shakespeare Plays," given at the SCA National Convention in San Antonio, Texas, in 1979; "Selected Styles of 'Acting' Applied to Reader's Theatre," at the ECA National Convention in Boston, Massachusetts; and "Reflections on Bertolt Brecht and Reader's Theatre," published in *Reader's Theatre News* in 1979.

His professional affiliations include membership in the Secondary School Theatre Association, the National Council of Teachers of English, the American Film Institute, the American Society for Theatre Research, the Eugene O'Neill Society, the American Studies Association, the College English Association, and the Ibsen Society of America.

ACKNOWLEDGMENTS

CONTENTS

PREFACE

Although it is not possible to personally thank all of the people responsible for the completion of this text, I should like to express my sincere appreciation to Florence Powell, who first kindled the flames of my love of theatre when I was an awkward gawky at Middletown (Ohio) High School; and to Donna and Peggy, who always seem to fan the fires of my imagination just as I suspect they are about to flicker and wane.

Credit must also be given in large measure to Michael Z. Murphy, whose difficult task as Assistant Editor provided the creative and theatrical movement for the selected scenes, and whose dedication and loyalty to this project resulted in the critical commentary necessary to keep the text from wandering; to Kevin Lee Allen, valued student and friend, whose artistic suggestions and sketches help to visualize what the selected scenes are all about; and to Ruth Rosen, whose genuine concern and enthusiasm for this project led me to embrace it with so much care.

A special acknowledgment is also due my students who, over the past ten years, have filled with wonder the performance classes in acting and Reader's Theatre that I have taught; and to Montclair State College and the Department of Speech and Theatre, who allow me to be myself as I cast about for interesting approaches to the teaching of scene study and playscript interpretation.

And to those young men and women who may read this text and be stimulated to realize their own creative potential, may I say good fortune, in all of your scene study and playscript interpretation, and may all of your classroom performances be truly inspired.

Montclair State College   GERALD LEE RATLIFF
January, 1980

The Theatre Student

LEARNING SCENES/BASIC ACTING

ARISTOPHANES TO ALBEE

TO THE INSTRUCTOR

The fundamental principle that brings together the selected scenes that comprise this sourcebook for performance is not at all simple, because the skill of perceptive play interpretation and scene study that translates into creative performance is not simple, and it may often appear to resist concise summary.

What does it mean to speak of the instructor's responsibility to encourage ideal conditions in which a beginning student may explore the creative dimensions of a given script; and is it a perspective upon the creative process itself that has any direct relationship to the reality of the present educational or academic structure?

What does it mean to speak of the instructor's obligation to promote self-discipline and stimulate desire so that a beginning student achieves a level of initial competence and self-satisfaction from his scene study, and in the process discovers the intricacies of interpretation and characterization that distinguish the art of performance?

These are the complex and intriguing questions that leap to mind at once as I cast about for the appropriate prefatory remarks to this volume; and they are questions that I shall undertake to answer here by way of a few observations, and certain presuppositions, that may put the instructor in mind of the suggested use of this performance sourcebook.

First, every instructor is well aware that beginning students have only one mutually compatible trait: the degree of stage fright exhibited in those first, awkward fruits of their classroom labors. They do not appear with the same level of experience, training, or knowledge; nor do they have the same maturity, dedication, or instant creativity. They have different assumptions and varying expectations, which must be satisfied if they are to enjoy a memorable and rewarding theatrical experience.

Much of the responsibility for alleviating the student's foremost fears and encouraging the ideal conditions in which creative exploration of the script may occur is surely that of the instructor. This sourcebook has been arranged to serve as an educational tool precisely to assist the instructor in meeting that responsibility. The scenes are conveniently grouped in historical sequence, from the classical interludes of the farcical Aristophanes to the absurd intrigues of the contemporary Albee, and successively progress in difficulty and design so that the student may build a foundation of self-confidence and accomplishment as he moves from one scene to another.

In addition, each scene includes the background knowledge that is necessary to enable the student to reach an understanding of the characters, and suggests performance goals and objectives that may help to crystalize that understanding.

Second, every instructor is sadly aware that beginning students have only a passing acquaintance with the dramatic literature of the theatre and may never have come in contact with the styles of performance that give accuracy and authenticity to an interpretation of the selected scene. As a consequence, the student has a limited vision of the historical dimensions of the play and a very superficial understanding of the attention to detail that is imperative to sustain believability in playing period plays.

Certainly it is the responsibility of the instructor to prepare a beginning student for an interpretation of the selected scene by pointing out the milieu in which the literature was conceived and the performance manners with which it was executed. This sourcebook provides that essential familiarity by an introductory essay for each scene that details the social climate and attitude of the times in which the play was written. There is also an introductory essay for each division of the sourcebook, which presents the performance blueprint necessary to recreate the scene in its original context. These brief essays also note the peculiar historical styles of movement, voice, and gesture associated with the plays and should encourage a lively discussion of the selected scenes in terms of their legendary staging techniques.

Third, every instructor knows what limited facilities are available for classroom performance and how much valuable time, which could be better spent in rehearsal, must be expended making clear the principles of stage movement, *i.e.*, blocking the scene. This sourcebook gives the instructor sufficient exemption from those arbitrary restrictions and problematic explanations by including a suggested directorial pattern of movement and action for each scene. The scheme for performance also places each scene in the typical classroom and utilizes generally available furnishings such as chairs, desks, or tables as recommended set pieces.

Finally, we come to a discussion of the role that the instructor should play in making this sourcebook available to the beginning student. Set aside a time for vocal and physical warm-ups that will prepare the student for the selected scene, and repeat basic exercises until a level of competence is achieved. Have a clear set of objectives in mind for each scene, but be flexible in approach so that the student may explore freely without a preconceived or rigid system of anticipated discoveries guiding the desired response. Be an active participant, but allow the student to experiment as much as possible. Insist on sufficient preparation and home study, perhaps supplemented by some basic library research, to encourage a more polished and informed approach to play interpretation and scene study; and cultivate the attitude that performance should be based on the historical background of the times and manners reflected in the play.

Above all, strike a compassionate balance between critical and artistic evaluation of the student performance so that the focus is on the theme of individual exploration, not on imitation. Perhaps these thoughts of Eleanora Duse, one of the most renowned of twentieth-century actresses, will provide inspiration to guide the instructor in the creative use of this sourcebook in the classroom:

To help, to continually help and share, that is the sum of all knowledge; that is the meaning of art.

TO THE STUDENT

This sourcebook of selected scenes, ranging from period to avant garde, is intended to acquaint the beginning student with the basic ingredients needed to suggest a polished and creative performance in the classroom. No attempt is made to categorize which approaches to performance or scene study are "best," but the text does stress that the beginning actor should suit his individual personality to the scenes and should be essentially subjective in deciding which of the suggested performance approaches might work most effectively given his own special talents or interests.

The sourcebook also anticipates many of the beginning actor's most frequent questions concerning movement, characterization, and style in a given scene by providing a blueprint for performance that spells out the fundamental principles of vocal and physical technique necessary to help create and sustain a believable role.

Before proceeding to a detailed analysis of what is involved in beginning scene study, however, it is necessary to point out some of the prerequisites of performance that the student actor must consider as he approaches the development and creation of a character for classroom presentation.

First, the beginning actor who engages in scene study and play interpretation should be knowledgeable, and that implies an understanding of the basic theatrical techniques and conventions that give credibility to any creative performance. Being knowledgeable also suggests a familiarity with the historical manners and customs associated with the style of the performance. This sourcebook makes that task easier by providing introductory essays detailing the times and events on which the selected scenes were based and defining the general characteristics of performance as they were exhibited in the period.

A second consideration is that the beginning actor should be disciplined, and that implies not only a self-controlled and orderly system of preparation and rehearsal, but also an efficiency of acting technique that will suggest to the audience that the final performance is spontaneous and true to life, not contrived or artificial. This sourcebook recognizes the beginning actor's limitations in terms of time available for scene study and rehearsal, and offers for consideration performance guidelines and character expectations that may be of value in the scene. The guidelines give the background information necessary to interpret the scene with historical accuracy, and the suggested character expectations point out performance possibilities that might give the presentation more vitality.

The sourcebook is also arranged so that the initial preparation and rehearsal periods lead naturally and easily to an investigation of the next scene in the sequence. This structure provides a series of "building blocks" with which the actor can construct an inspired and creative performance. In addition, the selected scenes are of such diversity, ranging in style from farces and interludes to melodramas and tragedies, that the beginning actor may evaluate his own emerging technique by testing its economy and efficiency in realizing the objectives spelled out as a prelude to each scene.

Another consideration is that the beginning actor should be innovative, and that implies that the play and the performance are given added dimension by original inventions and fresh interpretations. This essential ingredient of creativity, necessary for dynamic role-playing in the classroom performance, also suggests that the beginning actor has mastered the technical skills of stage characterization and that he has achieved a degree of uninhibited abandon to project himself as the fictitious character he is portraying. This sourcebook makes every effort to enlarge and enliven the actor's comic and dramatic potential for achieving meaningful characterization by incorporating performance ideas and character actions into the remarks that introduce the scenes.

The sourcebook also provides the basic patterns of movement most appropriate to highlight the character's objective in a given scene and encourages the beginning actor to experiment with the "character hints" as a sounding board for his own creative exploration in performance.

These final precepts are intended as reminders that the beginning actor's training program is a daily affair of keen observation and studied investigation. It should be obvious to the conscientious actor that the wider the range of experience and example from which he can draw, the more sensitive and complex the performance portrait is likely to be, and the more rewarding the creation. The beginning actor has a responsibility, therefore, to gather as much supporting material for his performance as possible so that he can strengthen and reinforce the chosen interpretation.

Sources of potential performance material might include books, television, movies, familiar persons, or even firsthand knowledge; but in all cases the material selected should be carefully woven into the performance so that it appears both natural and logical.

A truly inspired and creative performance also suggests that it is through the actor's own personality that the character has been molded and given life, and the primary performance goal for the beginning actor is to explore his own personality as a key to creative role-playing in the classroom. Perhaps the oft-quoted Polonius, Shakespeare's statesman of practical advice, most eloquently expresses what is desired of the beginning actor as he translates this sourcebook into creative performance:

To thine own self be true,
And it must follow as the night the day,
Thou canst not then be false to any man.

Act I

ON PLAYING PERIOD SCENES

The actor's basic approach to playing period plays depends upon his knowledge of the historical times in which the play was written and upon his own personality and persuasion.

Having gathered all of the information available regarding the performance style of the selected period, including vocal and physical demands, the beginning actor reveals his preparation by incorporating the documented traits and mannerisms into an interpretation of the role that suggests both the period and the character being portrayed.

But because the actor is also a creative artist, he must not only faithfully reproduce the historical style but must also compliment that creation with personal traits and mannerisms that help to reinforce the authenticity of the portrait.

That is not to say, however, that the actor merely does his research, "copies" what he has observed or discovered, and then submits it to the audience for comparison with the original. To take this approach to playing period plays would undoubtedly result in a static, uninspired performance that would neither mirror the historical times nor reflect the skill of the performer.

Perhaps that is the warning Shakespeare had in mind in his advice to the actors in Hamlet's now famous Players' speech:

. . . Suit the action to the word, the word to the action, with this special observance, that you o'erstep not the modesty of nature; for anything so overdone is from the purpose of playing, whose end, both at the first and now, was and is to hold, as 'twere, the mirror up to nature, to show virtue her own feature, scorn her own image, and the very age and body of the time his form and pressure. . . .

(III, ii)

Shakespeare's central point, that the actor should perform in a fashion that is both natural and credible for the time in which he lives, is the desired approach to be taken in performing the scenes that follow.

The beginning actor is asked to translate the given facts, as noted in the introduction to each period scene, into a performance that is representative of the actual patterns of behavior observed in the society of the times, and to remain faithful to this source so that the audience may glimpse the suggested historical style in performance.

To help the beginning actor communicate the style desired to represent the period,

7

performance hints and basic movement patterns are included for each scene. There are also enough clues provided in the staging devices and the comic bits of business that reveal character to stimulate further exploration.

Before proceeding to an examination of the individual scenes, however, it might be useful to point out some of the historical dimensions that could be used creatively in the classroom situation.

Lysistrata, for example, encourages the use of masks and bed sheets to suggest the historical period; and the current fashion of high-soled shoes is an excellent example of the classical *cothornus,* worn to elevate the ancient performer and to give stature to his character. An interesting convention of the historical times that might stimulate the audience reception of this amusing and daring episode might be the casting of men in the women's roles and the use of excessive padding to disguise the impersonation. There is also the historically accurate practice of staging the scene outdoors, with the audience seated on a sloping hill-side.

Both *She Stoops to Conquer* and *The School for Scandal,* representative of the "comedy of manners" that satirizes the foibles of high society, allow for ornamental jewelry, wigs, long gowns, and sport coats to suggest the elegant dress of the period. Tea and cakes may also be served to permit the performers to display their social graces and good taste. There is even the opportunity to add period music and to perform graceful historical dances.

If facilities are available, *The Importance of Being Earnest* may be performed in a patio or small waiting room environment, with the audience arranged on three sides. The performers, like those in the previously noted comedy of manners, may wear their finest dress clothes and add such accessories as fans, walking sticks, snuff boxes, or handkerchiefs to punctuate the humor of the dialogue.

Fashion may also be taken from its suggested environment and placed in a lounge or a small music chamber to help suggest the historical period. Some attempt should be made, however, to convey the impression that these characters are not truly sophisticated and refined and that their airs and speech are mere disguises. A good approach might be to occasionally mispronounce a French phrase, to dress extravagantly, or wear mismatched socks.

Regardless of the approach taken, the beginning actor must make certain that he is seen and heard by the audience. Period plays in particular demand that the performer face the audience whenever possible and present his character in a direct manner; perhaps because the majority of period characters are so frankly theatrical, there is never a need to be realistic.

It is also important for the beginning actor to have excellent diction and projection so that he can be clearly understood. Most of the humor of period plays is found in the wit of the dialogue, and the beginning actor should pronounce his words precisely so that the audience does not miss the intended joke.

A final word of caution in playing period plays is the necessity for physical movements to be fluid, well executed, and energetic. Period plays usually employ movement to reinforce or highlight the humor of the dialogue, and it should become an extension of what the dialogue suggests about the character's attitude or mood.

Staging

It is necessary for the beginning actor to know the tools and terminology of his trade, just as it is necessary for the musician to know the notes of the musical scale. This elementary diagram is provided to identify the specific areas of the playing space and to serve as a guide for the stage movement that is included for each scene. The area closest to the audience is called *downstage;* the area farthest from the audience is called *upstage.* Both upstage and downstage areas extend across the width of the playing area.

The area in the middle of the playing space is called *center;* it is the most prominent because it commands the greatest visual attention from the audience. Stage areas *left* and *right* are determined as the actor's left or right as he faces the audience.

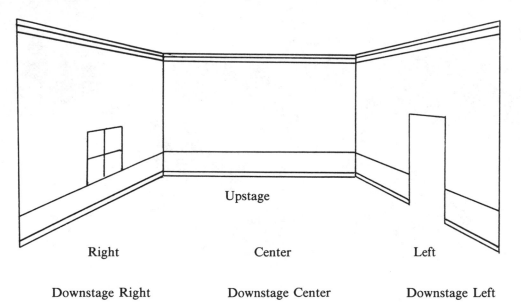

Upstage

Right   Center   Left

Downstage Right   Downstage Center   Downstage Left

FROM

Lysistrata (411 B.C.)
by ARISTOPHANES
adapted by GERALD LEE RATLIFF

By its very nature, coming as it does after epic and lyric poetry and still later than tragedy, classical "Old Comedy" enjoys much of the liberty of choice in subject matter and license of method and approach that mark present-day satire and burlesque.

The range and variety of subjects treated suggests a frank, uncompromising spirit of ribald humor and reckless high spirits. Indeed, whatever lends itself to satire is instantly seized upon for caricature. Eccentric and grotesque personalities are crudely parodied, social vices are quickly embraced, and pomposity and virtue are savagely ridiculed.

Lysistrata

An unchecked freedom of speech and suggestive language that is both harsh and vulgar also is found within the historical period. But it must not be forgotten that such language and license were part of the expected good fun, and that such burlesque humor was forbidden to women and children, who were initially barred from theatrical performances.

In terms of plot and action, this comedy is rather simple and unified. To force the men to stop the war between Athens and Sparta, which has raged for more than twenty years, Lysistrata urges the women of Greece to engage in a "sex strike" until the men agree to sue for peace. Although the women are at first reluctant, they finally agree and immediately capture the sacred Acropolis, forcing the men to surrender and make peace with Sparta.

In playing the scene the actor should grossly exaggerate the movement and action, suggesting the animation and vitality of the characters. The historical period also demands that the actor have at his command an arsenal of formalized gestures, stylized facial expressions, and well-developed pitch range.

Above all, the actor should not be timid or squeamish in executing the stage directions; it is part of the classical tradition for comic performers to engage in amusing insults and innuendo with the audience. This is especially true in the portrayal of Lysistrata, who should emerge as a crafty, blustering woman of incredible strength and will.

Cast:

> Lysistrata
> Calocine
> Voluptia

Scene:

> Athens. A public square in early morning.

ACT I

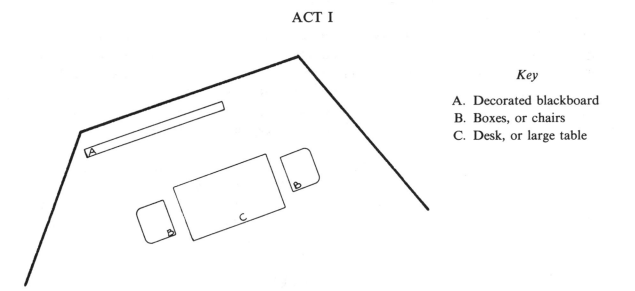

Key

A. Decorated blackboard
B. Boxes, or chairs
C. Desk, or large table

If space permits, this scene may also
be played on the floor level without set pieces.

The scene opens with Lysistrata discovered asleep upon the thymele, or sacred altar, snoring loudly. She had been awaiting the tardy arrival of some Athenian women summoned to the public square before sunrise to discuss a strategy for ending the Peloponnesian War.

Lysistrata's primary concern in the episode is to rouse the women's moral indignation and sense of outrage and to provoke them to engage in a marital strike that might bring the absent men home. She is not above intrigue, deception, or insult to achieve her aim.

Pacing of the scene should be rapid, especially on the initial series of entrances and exits by Calocine and the surprise appearance of Voluptia; and there should be frequent movement toward the audience to draw them into the action or to share confidences with them.

[1] Moans as in a dream.

[2] Sits up, then lies down.

[3] Sits up.

[4] Sees audience, jumps from the thymele and crosses down left.

[5] Crosses to down right.

[6] Places right hand on heart, left hand in air.

[7] Crosses to thymele and steps on it, using the right chair as a step.

[8] Squats and pounds thymele with fist.

[9] Pounds again.

[10] Stands.

[11] Squats.

[12] Gets on all fours.

[13] Wiggles rump.

[14] Flicks tongue at audience.

[15] Gets on knees.

[16] Pounds thymele.

[17] Pounds harder.

[18] Pounds even harder, and opens mouth to speak.

[19] Rushes on from down right and moves to right of thymele.

[20] Rushes down right, and returns quickly.

[21] Tweaks her nose.

LYSISTRATA: [1] Soft, [2] who goes there? By Athene, I could have sworn I heard the women come! O, [3] I must have dreamed it all. That it should come to this: asleep here all the long night in order to greet my sisters of Greece, who speed to assist me in a most daring plan to end the war which has ravaged our lands for thirty years!

O, [4] good morning to you, gentle Athenians! By Apollo, you have risen early to witness this spectacle! But why do you sit there with folded arms and knitted brows, while all around you Greece pulses and throbs? O, [5] now I see! 'Tis no small wonder. Most of you be men! But that is wise and to the point. For it is to you we would speak when all have come together here. By Eros, [6] it is an omen sure!

O, [7] sweet friends, listen to the wise counsel I am about to impart to you and take care that it is not lost upon you. 'Twould be the work of vulgar spectators if that were so; not that of such an audience as this, [8] by Jupiter! Lend me your ears if you love frank speaking. If you do not love frank speaking, stick your foot in your ear until I am done![9]

To be blunt, [10] men are like children twice over and it is far more fitting to soundly chastise them than to beat them; for there is more excuse for their faults! That is why I summon the women of Greece here this very morning. Our leadership is in fumbling hands. They are incompetent and impotent. [11] They press too hard and are now overextended. They force affairs, [12] come late, and their efforts are piecemeal to say the least. [13] They do not discharge their obligations, will not give an inch, and their tongues [14] are like double-edged swords.

And, [15] O how they love wars! They come grunting and humping home from the hunt, throw a raw piece of meat at you, bark a command or two, and expect the poor wife to sit up and beg like a common cur! O, [16] a plague [17] on the blanket infantry![18]

CALOCINE: Lysistrata, [19] I am come! It is time!

LYSISTRATA: Away with you! I have not yet reached my climax!

CALOCINE: [20] But you know the ancient proverb: "Speedy execution is greatly esteemed by the public."

LYSISTRATA: I know the ancient proverb, [21] twit! But I have not yet set sail all that is writ down for me. The playwright will

[22] Disapproves behind thymele. There is much noise, then a large manuscript is thrown out. Lysistrata reappears, disheveled.

[23] Flips through the manuscript, which is oversized and labeled "SCRIPT."

[24] Slams it closed.

[25] Struggles to top of thymele.

[26] Exits down right.

[27] Looks for a line in the manuscript.

[28] Tosses it up center, and stands.

[29] Kneels in prayer.

[30] Sees a particular man in audience.

[31] Jumps off thymele and crosses to him, pointing.

[32] Spies another man in audience left, and crosses down right to him.

[33] Snores grotesquely.

[34] Tiptoes quickly left.

[35] Pantomimes delivery of tray down right.

[36] Holds invisible head and coos.

[37] Crosses to right of thymele.

[38] Pounds.

[39] Pounds.

[40] Stands facing down with legs spread, hands on hips.

[41] Begins to swagger from down left to down right.

[42] Rushes on from down right and falls in behind Lysistrata.

[43] Points to up right door.

be at wit's end if I do not reach my climax! [22] He bids me here to lay the men low, and to weave a seductive web to entrap them.

CALOCINE: [23] Can't he weave his own web, and allow us to get down to our parts?

LYSISTRATA: Tis not a man's art! [24] Besides, it is well known that he writes his Prologues in a limping meter and does not run erect until half way home.

CALOCINE: How far is he from home now?

LYSISTRATA: [25] To judge from the sweetness of his words, I would say just above the hill of Pisander.

CALOCINE: Stick to him, then. I shall come again when he is in hand behind the door.[26]

LYSISTRATA: Now, [27] where was I? O, yes. [28] And how his moods change without rhyme or reason. If a man is to be believed, a woman is a plague on him! If a man is to be believed, through us come all his troubles, quarrels, disputes, frustrations and griefs! But, sweet sisters, if we are truly such a pest, why does he court us? [29] Why, by Aphrodite, does he marry us?

[30] You, sir. [31] If your wife goes out and you meet her away from the house, why do you fly into a fury? Ought you not rather to rejoice and give thanks to Zeus, for the pest has disappeared and you will no longer have her about the house? [32] And you, sir. When your wife falls asleep at a friend's house from too much wine or too much sporting, [33] why do you carry her home and then tip-toe [34] round the house so as not to wake this pest? [35] Why do you bring her breakfast in bed? [36] Why do you hold her head and put cold cloth to her face? Should you not have been glad that the pest nodded off?

O, [37] by Menelaos, tis true! [38] Tis true! [39] If we but seat ourselves at the window each one of you cranes his neck to see the pest! If we but stand in the doorway [40] each one of you walks up and down, [41] down and up, strutting like a proud peacock to see the pest!

CALOCINE: Lysistrata, [42] Lysistrata! By Poseidon, I am come again!

LYSISTRATA: Away! Away with you again! I am just now reaching my climax!

CALOCINE: Before you reach home?

LYSISTRATA: [43] I am at the front door this very minute!

[44] Sits on ground extreme down right.

[45] Stops pacing and rushes to above thymele for script. Audience sees only her head as she flips through it, and then leaves it on thymele.

[46] Crosses down center for a very formal delivery.

[47] Shudders with desire.

[48] Regains composure with some difficulty.

[49] Points an accusing finger.

[50] Rushes to her so quickly that Lysistrata is propelled down left by the impact.

[51] Crosses to script.

[52] Rushes to her and slams it shut, catching Lysistrata's hand inside.

[53] Removes hand and shakes it in pain.

[54] Begins to exit down right. Turns and then exits.

[55] Her hand still hurts.

[56] A long pause in which she tries to gesture Calocine on from the wings.

[57] From wings.

[58] Still from wings.

[59] Crosses down center for formal delivery.

[60] Opens mouth to speak but forgets lines. Dives for script and reads from center of thymele.

[61] Throws script upstage of thymele, then mounts it. Squints into distance and waits.

[62] Enters very slowly. She overacts very badly.

CALOCINE: I hope the door is not locked, [44] by Ajax!

LYSISTRATA: Now, [45] where am I? O, yes. This part of the Prologue is so dear to me that I have committed it to memory. No need for reference here.

Women of Athens, [46] do you remember how long it has been? O, [47] no, sisters not that! [48] Do you remember how many peaceful moments you have known? O, [49] no, my dainties, not that! Do you remember the beauty and serenity of life in Greece before the men grew fond of war? Yes, commrades, that's it!

Well, by a stroke of inspiration I have devised an ingenious strategy to secure the much-needed salvation of Greece. And here is the plan. I propose to call all of the women of Greece to arms, and to invite representatives of our sex to meet here this very morning so that we may resolve to end the war by . . .

CALOCINE: Lysistrata, [50] this is the last time I come! If you have not reached your climax by this time it is plain that the playwright did not reach his either!

LYSISTRATA: [51] But he seized every favorable opportunity. He advanced every new position. I have it here from his own mouth.

CALOCINE: Hold, [52] Lysistrata! Or the spectators will get wind of it! Remember what the ancients teach: "Whatever would offend is best left unsaid."

LYSISTRATA: Right, [53] by Artemis! But how shall we begin!

CALOCINE: [54] At the beginning! I shall run on, again, and you shall tell me of the ingenious plan you have devised to secure the peace of Greece.

LYSISTRATA: Right, [55] by Hymen![56]

CALOCINE: Well?[57]

LYSISTRATA: Well, what?

CALOCINE: [58] Thank the spectators and then be off! You have already overstayed your welcome.

LYSISTRATA: [59] Ladies and gentlemen, thank you for your indulgence! I must now shoot off to do the bidding of the playwright. Before I leave, however, I am sure that he would want me to say this to you. It was writ down before he misplaced his climax to the Prologue. [60] "Let the wise judge because of whatever is wise in this piece; and those who like a laugh by whatever has made them laugh. In this way I address most everyone here!" [61] Adieu, for now!

CALOCINE: [62] Women of Athens, behold! I have at no time spoken.

[63] Sits on center chair and sobs, with her face on Lysistrata's feet.

[64] Pulls her onto thymele. Eventually she is comforted.

[65] Calocine lifts her head abruptly.

[66] Pantomimes heaving boulders and adds elaborate sound effects.

[67] They do an elaborate secret handshake.

[68] Very loudly, as they move to the outside of the thymele.

[69] Leaps from behind the thymele. They pull her up with some effort.

[70] Strikes a sexy pose.

[71] And another one.

[72] She shimmies.

[73] They try to stop her but, like an electric current, they all shimmy.

[74] She stops, but they continue.

[75] Stops, leaps from thymele for the script and returns with it. They mumble over it for a while, while Calocine continues to shimmy.

[76] Reads from script.

[77] They both stare at Calocine.

[78] They grab Calocine to stop her. She is frenzied and appears as though she might begin again. They focus on her.

I do so now! For ourselves, we shall no doubt persuade our husbands to conclude a swift and lasting peace. But how, in the name of Athene, are we to cure the hot-blooded and frenzied Greek populace from waging war?[63]

LYSISTRATA: Have no fear, Calocine! [64] I have undertaken this very day to force our people to lay down their arms and to receive the message of peace. At dawn, under the pretense of sacrificing a goat to Hermes, the old women of Athens have gone afoot to seize the Acropolis! If all goes well, the citadel should be ours by high noon! Then, the men will have to mount *our* fortress if they want to reclaim the treasure of the temple. And it is at that time we shall force them to sue for peace!

CALOCINE: Well said, [65] Lysistrata! [66] And from our vantage point above the city we shall rain down fire upon their heads and rocks upon their swords!

LYSISTRATA: But come quickly, [67] commrade! You must now learn how to stand the test, to hold your own and to go forward without feeling fatigue in the long battle ahead. And so that you may prove fruitful in your quest, I have arranged for some special instruction. [68] Call forth Voluptia, fair peach of Athens! She shall instruct us all in the art of women's warfare![69]

CALOCINE: O, no! Not Voluptia! You're not going to believe this tale!

VOLUPTIA: O, [70] Ladies of Greece. You do me praise to call me forth from my labors to here instruct you in my special crafts. [71] I speak as one who has given much, and often, to her country. I speak as one who knows full well the secrets of formations, desirable positions, [72] size of reinforcements and all of the military chatter relating to involuntary movements [73] on the parts of our enemies.

CALOCINE: With all fifty of his Majesty's legions no doubt!

VOLUPTIA: For you, [74] however, I shall be brief! Come, sisters! Pain and suffering are yours. Accept them! You must be zealous and silent and endure! Why hoard for death your maidenhood?

LYSISTRATA: Voluptia, [75] that's the wrong speech!

VOLUPTIA: O, [76] by Pisander! Pardon me, sisters! My passion is such that I forget my purpose. Women of Greece, [77] if you would end the war and secure the peace for which you lay awake each night you must wipe all decency from your face! Steady, [78] sisters!

A dose of hellbore to give you a brainwash, that's what you

[79] Calocine starts but is stopped again.

[80] Lysistrata and Calocine sit on outer corners of thymele.

[81] Lines eyes as Lysistrata and Calocine pantomime the list.

[82] Fluff hair.

[83] Lipstick.

[84] Brow pencil.

[85] Veil faces with hands.

[86] Arm and leg ornaments.

[87] Sniff armpits.

[88] Points to Calocine.

[89] Pokes Lysistrata in ticklish places.

[90] Leads a parade around thymele as she demonstrates.

[91] All pantomime rouge application.

[92] Flexes her biceps.

[93] Gulps for air.

[94] On brink of collapse.

[95] Collapses.

[96] Raises her head.

[97] Grabs script.

[98] At center.

[99] Places one hand on it.

[100] Raises and places one hand on it.

[101] They smile. Then giggle. Then laugh. All exit with the script held high, up left.

need! And not the common stuff the apothecaries peddle in the marketplace either, but the special brand from Antigua! [79] Steady, [80] sisters!

Eyes [81] emphasized with kohl and [82] false hair, [83] painted lips and [84] lined brows! Wax and [85] Tarentine wraps, and earrings. Snake-winding [86] bracelets, anklets, chains and lockets! Steady, sisters! But no roses! O, by Pluto, no roses! [87] When they lose their fragrance both men and gods stay away, for the odor has a marvelous capacity to drive away all repose!

[88] What you don't possess by Nature you may acquire by imitation, and a little padding! And don't forget that a woman cannot possibly be loved without perfume! [89] So put it here and there and everywhere! [90] And when you walk spring forward with a light step. See, walk as I and men will gaze at you with wonder, their heads erect and their faces beaming with delight at the sight!

And don't forget to let your hands interlace, as though you were praying with each step! And, O, face without chalk! Remember, my dainties, for a woman [91] redness of face is the shining flower of charm. To rouge, my sweets, to rouge! But do not be harsh or frightening, and do not seal your beauty away in scarf or veil! O, sisters, throw off those nets that sore beset you, and reveal your loveliness!

CALOCINE: At last [92] she has hit upon something which strikes home!

VOLUPTIA: There's not a part of you but snares men to their doom! Love beckons in your eyes, [93] your mouths are songs of grace, your hands are scions of strength and flowers blossom in your cheeks! If you do not believe my craft, take up your mirror and see how your face has changed. O, [94] receive them with scented hair, in fragrant delicto at the half moon! O, my sweets, what a noble work of art is Woman![95]

[96] And don't forget to imitate the twelve postures of Cyrone!

LYSISTRATA: Come quickly, [97] sisters! While the fit of passion is upon us let each swear an inviolable oath of abstinence! [98] We will swear!

CALOCINE: [99] We will swear!

VOLUPTIA: [100] We will swear!

ALL: [101] We will swear!

FROM

She Stoops to Conquer (1773)
by OLIVER GOLDSMITH
edited by ARTHUR FRIEDMAN

The genteel comedy of the eighteenth century is usually characterized by its efforts to "teach a lesson" through an appeal to the emotions, and the characters are generally portrayed as either unduly good or unjustly evil. Playwrights often appear to have sacrificed dramatic reality in an attempt to depict virtue triumph over vice, and "private woes" are exhibited to arouse the spectator's pity and suspense before the typical melodramatic "happy ending."

Even the mildest mishap or the simplest happiness is treated with an admirable display of restraint, and as a result the characters often appear idiotic or selfish. They make their demands of each other and engage in the eternal battle of the sexes with vigor and zest, but beneath the convenient masks they wear each character is seemingly honest and delights in pointing out ridiculous pretensions or amusing flaws to the audience, usually in the form of an aside.

These scenes revolve around Young Marlow and Kate Hardcastle who, promised in marriage many years earlier, are now finally to meet. Marlow and his friend Hastings are on the way to the Hardcastle estate when they are met by Tony Lumpkin, Mrs. Hardcastle's rascally son by a previous marriage. They are deceived into believing that the Hardcastle estate is in reality a roadside inn, and upon arrival they begin to treat Mr. Hardcastle and his lovely daughter Kate as landlord and maid.

Kate takes advantage of the misunderstanding to observe the rigid code of behavior that Marlow supposedly follows and prepares to test him by posing as a carefree barmaid. A host of inept servants add to the general merriment, and the hilarious mistakes of the evening's encounter are resolved happily as the curtain falls.

In playing the scene the beginning actor should be able to convince the audience that he is enjoying his character's peculiar eccentricity and should never appear rude or ill-mannered. The mood of the scene demands gaiety and abandon, and there is a conversational tone to the teasing exchanges between Marlow and Miss Hardcastle.

Movement should be fluid and graceful, and the historical period suggests exaggerated posing and posturing by each of the characters. The verbal skirmishes should be handled with polite sensibility to reveal the social mores of the times, and there should be an attempt to "woo" with facial expressions.

Cast:

Mrs. Hardcastle
Hardcastle
Tony
Miss Hardcastle
Miss Neville

Scene:

A chamber in an old-fashioned house.

ACT I, Scene I

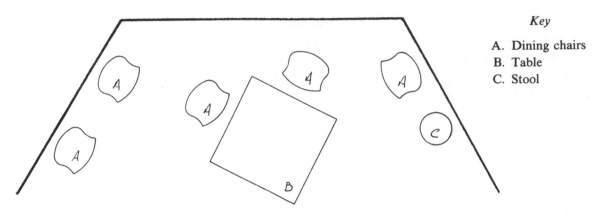

Key

A. Dining chairs
B. Table
C. Stool

As the scene opens, the Hardcastle household is in turmoil over the anticipated arrival of Young Marlow, the handsome and dashing gallant who is to present himself for approval in the impending marriage with the Hardcastles' beautiful daughter Kate.

There is an air of chaos and panic as the elder Hardcastles contemplate Kate's reaction to the as yet unrevealed betrothal, especially because she is so independent and self-willed. There is also the serious matter of what to do with Tony, Mrs. Hardcastle's son by a former marriage, so that he does not disrupt the marriage preparations with his usual pranks and mischief-making.

[1] Enters up left in a hurry and begins setting the room for dinner. Hardcastle holds up left for a moment, and then crosses to up left chair and sits.

[2] Moves up right chair to table and then moves down left chair to table.

[3] Circles up left and waves Hardcastle off chair, which she also places at table.

[4] Circling table very slowly from down left to down right, adjusting the chairs.

[5] Moves up left chair to end of table.

MRS. HARDCASTLE: I vow, [1] Mr. Hardcastle, you're very particular. [2] Is there a creature in the whole country, but ourselves, that does not take a trip to town now and then, to rub off the rust a little? [3] There's the two Miss Hoggs, and our neighbour, Mrs. Grigsby, go to take a month's polishing every winter.

HARDCASTLE: Ay, and bring back vanity and affectation to last them the whole year. I wonder why London cannot keep its own fools at home. In my time, the follies of the town crept slowly among us, but now they travel faster than a stage-coach. Its fopperies come down, not only as inside passengers, but in the very basket.

MRS. HARDCASTLE: Ay, [4] *your* times were fine times, indeed; you have been telling us of *them* for many a long year. Here we live in an old rumbling mansion, that looks for all the world like an inn, but that we never see company. [5] Our best visitors are old Mrs. Oddfish, the curate's wife, and little Cripplegate,

6 Crosses to her and slaps her on bottom.

7 Crosses down right.

8 Crosses down right in pursuit.

9 Retreats down left and sits on stool.

10 Sits at table in down right chair.

11 Rises and moves to table, where she takes chair at end of table and places it in original place up left.

12 Crosses to him. She waves him out of the chair and slides it under the table.

13 Crosses down left and sits.

14 Crosses to behind him and pats his shoulder.

15 Starts to rise, but she pushes him back down.

16 Pats him again.

17 Rises.

18 Pushes him down.

the lame dancing-master. And all our entertainments your old stories of Prince Eugene and the Duke of Marlborough. I hate such old-fashioned trumpery.

HARDCASTLE: 6 And I love it. I love every thing that's old: old books, old friends, old times, old manners, old wine; and, I believe, Dorothy, you'll own I have been pretty fond of an old wife.

MRS. HARDCASTLE: Lord, 7 Mr. Hardcastle, you're forever at your Dorothy's and your old wife's. You may be a Darby, but I'll be no Joan, I promise you. I'm not so old as you'd make me, by more than one good year. Add twenty to twenty, and make money of that.

HARDCASTLE: 8 Let me see; twenty added to twenty, makes just fifty and seven.

MRS. HARDCASTLE: It's false, 9 Mr. Hardcastle: I was but twenty when I was brought to bed of Tony, that I had by Mr. Lumpkin, my first husband; and he's not come to years of discretion yet.

HARDCASTLE: 10 Nor ever will, I dare answer for him. Ay, you have taught *him* finely.

MRS. HARDCASTLE: No matter, 11 Tony Lumpkin has a good fortune. My son is not to live by his learning. I don't think a boy wants much learning to spend fifteen hundred a year.

HARDCASTLE: Learning, quotha! A mere composition of tricks and mischief.

MRS. HARDCASTLE: Humour, 12 my dear: nothing but humour. Come, Mr. Hardcastle, you must allow the boy a little humour.

HARDCASTLE: 13 I'd sooner allow him a horse-pond. If burning the footmen's shoes, frightening the maids, and worrying the kittens, be humour, he has it. It was but yesterday he fastened my wig to the back of my chair, and when I went to make a bow, I popt my bald head in Mrs. Frizzle's face.

MRS. HARDCASTLE: 14 And am I to blame? The poor boy was always too sickly to do any good. A school would be his death. When he comes to be a little stronger, who knows what a year or two's Latin may do for him.

HARDCASTLE: Latin for him! 15 A cat and fiddle. No, no, the alehouse and the stable are the only schools he'll ever go to.

MRS. HARDCASTLE: Well, 16 we must not snub the poor boy now, for I believe we shan't have him long among us. Any body that looks in his face may see he's consumptive.

HARDCASTLE: 17 Ay, if growing too fat be one of the symptoms.

MRS. HARDCASTLE: 18 He coughs sometimes.

[19] Rises.

[20] Pushes him down.

[21] Tony enters in a rush and moves from up left to up right exit.

[22] Stops him at door, up right.

[23] Crosses down right.

[24] Crosses to him and feels forehead for a fever.

[25] Breaks away and moves down center.

[26] Finally able to rise.

[27] Holds down right.

[28] Sits on end of the table.

[29] Crosses to him.

[30] Leaps from table.

[31] Rushes to door and blocks passage with her arms.

[32] Turns to face her.

[33] Stamps her foot.

[34] Crosses to her and hugs her waist. He picks her up, kisses her, and removes her from the passageway for his exit. She follows him out in pursuit.

[35] Moves down left as Kate enters from up right in a backward movement, looking over her shoulder.

[36] Turns to see him as they both move center to hold hands.

[37] Pinches his cheeks.

[38] Pinches her cheeks.

HARDCASTLE: Yes, [19] when his liquor goes the wrong way.

MRS. HARDCASTLE: [20] I'm actually afraid of his lungs.

HARDCASTLE: And truly so am I; for he sometimes whoops like a speaking trumpet—O there he goes—. A very consumptive figure, truly.[21]

MRS. HARDCASTLE: Tony, [22] where are you going, my charmer? Won't you give papa and I a little of your company, lovee?

TONY: [23] I'm in haste, mother, I cannot stay.

MRS. HARDCASTLE: [24] You shan't venture out this raw evening, my dear: You look most shockingly.

TONY: I can't stay, [25] I tell you. The Three Pigeons expects me down every moment. There's some fun going forward.

HARDCASTLE: Ay; [26] the ale-house, the old place: I thought so.

MRS. HARDCASTLE: A low, [27] paltry set of fellows.

TONY: [28] No so low neither. There's Dick Muggins the exciseman, Jack Slang the horse doctor, Little Aminadab that grinds the music box, and Tom Twist that spins the pewter platter.

MRS. HARDCASTLE: Pray, [29] my dear, disappoint them for one night at least.

TONY: As for disappointing *them*, [30] I should not so much mind; but I can't abide to disappoint *myself.*

MRS. HARDCASTLE: [31] You shan't go.

TONY: I will, [32] I tell you.

MRS. HARDCASTLE: I say you shan't.[33]

TONY: [34] We'll see which is strongest, you or I.

HARDCASTLE: Ay, [35] there goes a pair that only spoil each other. But is not the whole age in a combination to drive sense and discretion out of doors? There's my pretty darling Kate; the fashions of the times have almost infected her too. By living a year or two in town, she is as fond of gauze, and French frippery, as the best of them.

[36] Blessings on my pretty innocence! Drest out as usual, my Kate. Goodness! What a quantity of superfluous silk hast thou got about thee, girl! I could never teach the fools of this age that the indigent world could be clothed out of the trimmings of the vain.

MISS HARDCASTLE: You know our agreement, [37] Sir. You allow me the morning to receive and pay visits, and to dress in my own manner; and in the evening, I put on my housewife's dress to please you.

HARDCASTLE: Well, [38] remember I insist on the terms of our

³⁹ Backs away a few steps.

⁴⁰ Moves to down left chair and pulls it away from table.

⁴¹ Sits.

⁴² Paces to down left then to up left, then to up right, and finally to down right.

⁴³ Moves two steps to him.

⁴⁴ Nods.

⁴⁵ Moves two steps to him.

⁴⁶ Nods.

⁴⁷ Moves two steps to him.

⁴⁸ Nods.

⁴⁹ Rushes to sit on his lap.

⁵⁰ Hugs her.

⁵¹ Leaps up and crosses down right.

⁵² Crosses to her and places arms around her shoulders.

⁵³ Kisses him on cheek.

agreement; and, by the bye, I believe I shall have occasion to try your obedience this very evening.

MISS HARDCASTLE: I protest, [39] Sir, I don't comprehend your meaning.

HARDCASTLE: Then, [40] to be plain with you, Kate, I expect the young gentleman I have chosen to be your husband from town this very day. [41] I have his father's letter, in which he informs me his son is set out, and that he intends to follow himself shortly after.

MISS HARDCASTLE: Indeed! [42] I wish I had known something of this before. Bless me, how shall I behave? It's a thousand to one I shan't like him; our meeting will be so formal, and so like a thing of business, that I shall find no room for friendship or esteem.

HARDCASTLE: Depend upon it, child, I'll never control your choice; but Mr. Marlow, whom I have pitched upon, is the son of my old friend, Sir Charles Marlow, of whom you have heard me talk so often. The young gentleman has been bred a scholar, and is designed for an employment in the service of his country. I am told he's a man of an excellent understanding.

MISS HARDCASTLE: Is he?[43]

HARDCASTLE: [44] Very generous.

MISS HARDCASTLE: [45] I believe I shall like him.

HARDCASTLE: Young and brave.[46]

MISS HARDCASTLE: [47] I'm sure I shall like him.

HARDCASTLE: And very handsome.[48]

MISS HARDCASTLE: My dear Papa, [49] say no more. He's mine, I'll have him.

HARDCASTLE: [50] And to crown all, Kate, he's one of the most bashful and reserved young fellows in all the world.

MISS HARDCASTLE: Eh! [51] you have frozen me to death again. That word reserved, has undone all the rest of his accomplishments. A reserved lover, it is said, always makes a suspicious husband.

HARDCASTLE: On the contrary, [52] modesty seldom resides in a breast that is not enriched with nobler virtues. It was the very feature in his character that first struck me.

MISS HARDCASTLE: He must have more striking features to catch me, I promise you. However, if he be so young, so handsome, and so every thing, as you mention, I believe he'll do still. I think I'll have him.[53]

⁵⁴ Takes her hand.

⁵⁵ Breaks away and crosses to above chair, down left.

⁵⁶ Crosses to her, and kisses her cheek as he exits up left.

⁵⁷ Collapses in chair down left, quickly rises, and then tries another chair until at the conclusion of the speech all the chairs have been pulled from the table and she is sitting in chair down right.

⁵⁸ Enters up right.

⁵⁹ Rises and crosses to her. They exchange kisses.

⁶⁰ They cross down right, arm in arm.

⁶¹ Crosses to stool and sits.

⁶² Pushes up right chair under the table.

⁶³ Pushes down right chair under the table.

⁶⁴ Pushes up left chair under the table.

⁶⁵ Pushes down left chair under the table and crosses to her.

⁶⁶ Rises.

HARDCASTLE: Ay, ⁵⁴ Kate, but there is still an obstacle. It's more than an even wager, he may not have *you.*

MISS HARDCASTLE: My dear Papa, ⁵⁵ why will you mortify one so? Well, if he refuses, instead of breaking my heart at his indifference, I'll only break my glass for its flattery. Set my cap to some newer fashion, and look out for some less difficult admirer.

HARDCASTLE: Bravely resolved! ⁵⁶ In the meantime I'll go prepare the servants for his reception; as we seldom see company they want as much training as a company of recruits, the first day's muster.

MISS HARDCASTLE: Lud, ⁵⁷ this news of Papa's puts me all in a flutter. Young, handsome; these he put last; but I put them foremost. Sensible, good-natured; I like all that. But then reserved, and sheepish, that's much against him. Yet can't he be cured of his timidity, by being taught to be proud of his wife? Yes, and can't I—But I vow I'm disposing of the husband, before I have secured the lover.⁵⁸

I'm glad you're come, ⁵⁹ Neville, my dear. Tell me, ⁶⁰ Constance, how do I look this evening? Is there any thing whimsical about me? Is it one of my well looking days, child? Am I in face today?

MISS NEVILLE: Perfectly, my dear. Yet now I look again—bless me!—sure no accident has happened among the canary birds or the gold fishes. Has your brother or the cat been meddling? Or has the last novel been too moving?

MISS HARDCASTLE: No; nothing of this. ⁶¹ I have been threatened—I can scarce get it out—I have been threatened with a lover.

MISS NEVILLE: ⁶² And his name—.

MISS HARDCASTLE: Is Marlow.

MISS NEVILLE: Indeed!⁶³

MISS HARDCASTLE: The son of Sir Charles Marlow.

MISS NEVILLE: As I live, ⁶⁴ the most intimate friend of Mr. Hastings, *my* admirer. They are never asunder. I believe you must have seen him when we lived in town.

MISS HARDCASTLE: Never.

MISS NEVILLE: ⁶⁵ He's a very singular character, I assure you. Among women of reputation and virtue, he is the modestest man alive; but his acquaintance give him a very different character among creatures of another stamp: you understand me?

MISS HARDCASTLE: An odd character, ⁶⁶ indeed. I shall never

[67] Crosses down center.

[68] Extends her hand.

[69] Crosses to her and takes her hand.

[70] Crosses up right.

[71] Crosses up left.

[72] Crosses up center.

[73] Crosses up center to meet her.

[74] They hold hands and kiss.

[75] Leads her off, up right.

be able to manage him. What shall I do? Pshaw, [67] think no more of him, but trust to occurrences for success. But how goes on your own affair, my dear, has my mother been courting you for my brother Tony, as usual?[68]

MISS NEVILLE: [69] I have just come from one of our agreeable tête-a-têtes. She has been saying a hundred tender things, and setting off her pretty monster as the very pink of perfection.

MISS HARDCASTLE: And her partiality is such, [70] that she actually thinks him so. A fortune like yours is no small temptation. Besides, as she has the sole management of it, I'm not surprised to see her unwilling to let it go out of the family.

MISS NEVILLE: A fortune like mine, [71] which chiefly consists in jewels, is no such mighty temptation. But at any rate if my dear Hastings be but constant, I make no doubt to be too hard for her at last. However, I let her suppose that I am in love with her son, and she never once dreams that my affections are fixed upon another.

MISS HARDCASTLE: [72] My good brother holds out stoutly, and I could almost love him for hating you so.

MISS NEVILLE: [73] It is a good-natured creature at bottom, and I'm sure would wish to see me married to any body but himself. But my aunt's bell rings for our afternoon walk round the improvements. Come on! [74] Courage is necessary as our affairs are critical.

MISS HARDCASTLE: Would it were bed time and all were well.[75]

Having discovered Tony's practical joke in directing Marlow to the Hardcastle estate as though it were a common inn, Miss Hardcastle decides to present herself to him as a barmaid. Her purpose, for which she disguises both her voice and her dress, is to observe his true nature and character.

She is also concerned with the truth of the rumors that suggest Marlow is much attracted to ladies who are rather free in their affections and their intimacy with young gentlemen; and she plans to use this opportunity to test the truth of the gossip by teasing him.

Marlow himself is recovering from the embarrassment of having been so nervous and frightened at their first meeting, several hours earlier, that he could not once glance up during the interview. So during this scene Marlow tries to recover his confidence with women by pursuing what he assumes to be a flirtatious young woman of some experience in romance and intrigue.

The tone of the scene is one of initial attraction and then amorous conquest, as both Marlow and Miss Hardcastle fence seductively with words and movement. There should also be a suggestion of coy innocence and playful teasing as each character tries to control the action with witty remarks before they abandon the roles they have assumed and become more sincere at the conclusion of the scene.

ACT III, SCENE I

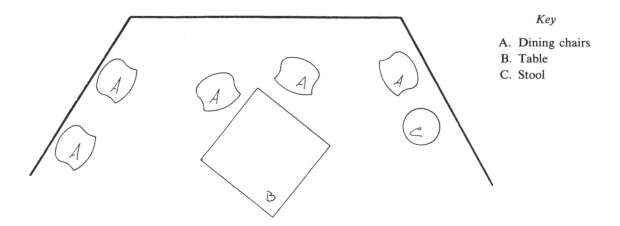

Key

A. Dining chairs
B. Table
C. Stool

Cast:

   Miss Hardcastle
   Marlow
   Hardcastle

Scene:

   Later that evening in another part of the house.

[1] Enters from up right with hands over ears and climbs on top of the table, only to lie on his back.

[2] From offstage left.

[3] Rises quickly to a sitting position and indicates to the audience that the voice is familiar.

[4] From offstage left again, but louder.

[5] Jumps from the table and moves down right, imitating the face to the audience.

[6] Enters up left slowly, displaying the same face just described to the audience.

[7] Moves slowly to the table.

[8] Crosses to stool down left and sits.

[9] Crosses down center.

[10] Stands on stool.

[11] Crosses to him and stares into his eyes.

MARLOW: [1] What a bawling in every part of the house; I have scarce a moment's repose. If I go to the best room, there I find my host and his story. If I fly to the gallery, there we have my hostess with her curtsy down to the ground. I have at last got a moment to myself, and now for recollection.

MISS HARDCASTLE: Did you call, [2] Sir? Did your honour call?

MARLOW: As for Miss Hardcastle, [3] she's too grave and sentimental for me.

MISS HARDCASTLE: Did your honour call?[4]

MARLOW: No, [5] child. Besides from the glimpse I had of her, I think she squints.

MISS HARDCASTLE: I'm sure, [6] Sir, I heard the bell ring.[7]

MARLOW: No, [8] no! (Aside.) I have pleased my father, however, by coming down, and I'll tomorrow please myself by returning.

MISS HARDCASTLE: [9] Perhaps the other gentleman called, Sir.

MARLOW: I tell you, [10] no.

MISS HARDCASTLE: I should be glad to know, [11] Sir. We have such a parcel of servants.

MARLOW: No, no, I tell you. Yes, child, I think I did call. I

[12] Retreats a few steps down center, shaking her head from side to side in a playful mood.

[13] Leaps from stool and moves a few steps toward her.

[14] Shakes her head violently.

[15] Moves a few steps toward her.

[16] Shakes her head violently.

[17] Crosses to down left end of table and sits.

[18] Crosses to stool and moves it to him, placing it at his feet.

[19] Sits.

[20] Stops shaking her head.

[21] Takes her chin in his hand.

[22] Leans backward and falls off the stool as he tries to kiss her.

[23] Struggles to regain her poise.

[24] Loses her cap and crawls under the table.

[25] Pokes head out.

[26] Rises and crosses down right.

[27] Turns to her.

wanted—I wanted—I vow child, you are vastly handsome.

MISS HARDCASTLE: O la, [12] Sir, you'll make one asham'd.

MARLOW: [13] Never saw a more sprightly malicious eye. Yes, yes, my dear, I did call. Have you got any of your—a—what d'ye call it in the house?

MISS HARDCASTLE: No, [14] Sir, we have been out of that these ten days.

MARLOW: One may call in this house, [15] I find, to very little purpose. Suppose I should call for a taste, just by way of trial, of the nectar of your lips; perhaps I might be disappointed of that too.

MISS HARDCASTLE: Nectar! [16] nectar! That's a liquor there's no call for in these parts. French, I suppose. We keep no French wines here, Sir.

MARLOW: Of true English growth, [17] I assure you.

MISS HARDCASTLE: [18] Then it's odd I should not know it. We brew all sorts of wines in this house, and I have lived here these eighteen years.[19]

MARLOW: Eighteen years! Why one would think, child, you kept the bar before you were born. How old are you?

MISS HARDCASTLE: O! [20] Sir, I must not tell my age. They say women and music should never be dated.

MARLOW: To guess at this distance, [21] you can't be much above forty. Yet nearer I don't think so much. By coming close to some women they look younger still; but when we come very close indeed.[22]

MISS HARDCASTLE: Pray, [23] Sir, keep your distance. One would think you wanted to know one's age as they do horses, by mark of mouth.[24]

MARLOW: I protest, child, you use me extremely ill. If you keep me at this distance, how is it possible you and I can ever be acquainted?

MISS HARDCASTLE: [25] And who wants to be acquainted with you? I want no such acquaintance, not I. I'm sure you did not treat Miss Hardcastle that was here awhile ago in this obstropalous manner. I'll warrant me, before her you look'd dash'd, and kept bowing to the ground, and talk'd, for all the world, as if you was before a justice of peace.

MARLOW: Egad! [26] (Aside.) She has hit it, sure enough. (To her.) In awe of her, [27] child? Ha! ha! ha! A mere awkward, squinting thing, no, no. I find you don't know me. I laugh'd, and ralled her a little; but I was unwilling to be too severe. No, I could not be too severe, *curse me!*

[28] Rises and moves stool to its original position down left.

[29] Crosses to right of table and makes a series of three quick bows.

[30] Crosses to table to resume search for the lost cap.

[31] Sits in down right chair.

[32] Crawling on all fours.

[33] Crawls under the table again.

[34] Rises and crosses to the table.

[35] Reclines on the table to watch the search.

[36] Bangs her head on the table.

[37] Lies on belly to watch the search, facing the audience.

[38] Trying to free herself from under the table, she bangs her head again.

[39] Enters in a hurry upstage left as Miss Hardcastle is backing out from beneath the table with the cap in her hands.

[40] Moves centerstage.

[41] Crosses to him.

MISS HARDCASTLE: O! [28] then, Sir, you are a favourite, I find, among the ladies?

MARLOW: Yes, my dear, a great favourite. And yet, hang me, I don't see what they find in me to follow. At the Ladies Club in town, I'm called their agreeable Rattle. Rattle, child, is not my real name, but one I'm known by. [29] My name is Solomons. Mr. Solomons, my dear, at your service.

MISS HARDCASTLE: Hold, [30] Sir; you were introducing me to your club, not to yourself. And you're so great a favourite there, you say?

MARLOW: [31] Yes, my dear. There's Mrs. Mantrap, Lady Betty Blackleg, the Countess of Sligo, Mrs. Langhorns, old Miss Biddy Buckskin, and your humble servant, keep up the spirit of the place.

MISS HARDCASTLE: [32] Then it's a very merry place, I suppose.

MARLOW: Yes, as merry as cards, suppers, wines, and old women can make us.

MISS HARDCASTLE: And their agreeable Rattle, [33] ha! ha! ha!

MARLOW: Egad! (Aside.) I don't quite like this chit. [34] She looks knowing, methinks. (To her.) You laugh, child.[35]

MISS HARDCASTLE: [36] I can't but laugh to think what time they all have for minding their work or their family.

MARLOW: [37] (Aside.) All's well, she doesn't laugh at me. (To her.) Do *you* ever work, child?

MISS HARDCASTLE: Ay, [38] sure. There's not a screen or a quilt in the whole house but what can bear witness to that.

MARLOW: Odso! Then you must show me your embroidery. I embroider and draw patterns myself a little. If you want to have a judge of your work you must apply to me.

MISS HARDCASTLE: Ay, but the colours don't look well by candle light. You shall see all in the morning.

MARLOW: And why not now, my angel? Such beauty fires beyond the power of resistance. Pshaw! the father here! My old luck: I never nick'd seven that I did not throw ames ace three times following.

HARDCASTLE: So, [39] madam! So I find *this* is your *modest* lover. This is your humble admirer that kept his eyes fixed on the ground, and only ador'd at humble distance. Kate, [40] Kate, art thou not asham'd to deceive your father so?

MISS HARDCASTLE: Never trust me, [41] dear papa, but he's still the modest man I first took him for, you'll be convinced of it as well as I.

42 Crosses to left of table to face Marlow.

43 Crosses to right of table to face Marlow, who lies down to nap during this exchange of dialogue.

44 Bangs the table for emphasis.

45 Bangs the table for emphasis.

46 Crosses down to centerstage.

47 Crosses to him.

48 Exits in a hurry up left. Marlow falls asleep, snoring loudly.

49 Crosses to the table. Marlow snores louder.

50 Exits in a hurry up left. Marlow is left alone, snoring, as the curtain falls.

HARDCASTLE: 42 By the hand of my body I believe his impudence is infectious! Didn't I see him seize your hand? Didn't I see him hawl you about like a milk maid? And now you talk of his respect and his modesty, forsooth!

MISS HARDCASTLE: 43 But if I shortly convince you of his modesty, that he has only the faults that will pass off with time, and the virtues that will improve with age, I hope you'll forgive him.

HARDCASTLE: 44 The girl would actually make one run mad! I tell you I'll not be convinced. I am convinced. He has scarcely been three hours in the house, and he has already encroached on all my prerogatives. You may like his impudence, and call it modesty. But my son-in-law, madam, must have very different qualifications.

MISS HARDCASTLE: Sir, 45 I ask but this night to convince you.

HARDCASTLE: 46 You shall not have half the time, for I have thoughts of turning him out this very hour.

MISS HARDCASTLE: 47 Give me that hour then, and I hope to satisfy you.

HARDCASTLE: Well, 48 an hour let it be then. But I'll have no trifling with your father. All fair and open do you mind me.

MISS HARDCASTLE: I hope, 49 Sir, you have ever found that I considered your commands as my pride; for your kindness is such, that my duty as yet has been inclination.50

FROM

The School for Scandal (1977)
by RICHARD BRINSLEY SHERIDAN

As the best example of the English comedy of manners, this witty and "upper-class" comedy ridicules the conventional deportment of wealthy people who live within the narrow restraints of a rigid and artificial social code. The main action of the play is set against the frivolous background of a private "school for scandal," in which a circle of malicious men and women destroy reputation and ruin character while politely sipping afternoon tea.

Lady Sneerwell and her entourage of hypocritical scandalmongers set the tone of the play, and their shallowness provides the comic impulse for Sir Peter Teazle and his young wife to learn the valuable lesson that virtue is its own reward.

In such a shallow society as this, polished and highly elegant behavior assumes prime importance, and values such as morality and decency are easily dismissed or brushed aside. Although there are some characters, Maria for example, who hold old-fashioned principles of moderation and humility, the majority are more concerned with the vogue for sentimentalism epitomized by the comic villain Joseph Surface, who is admired for his overindulgence in emotional conversation and for sprinkling his social commentary with thought-provoking moral proverbs.

In playing the scenes the actor should convey a light and delicate sense of movement, punctuated with elegant bows or deep curtsies, and an air of chic sophistication. Accompanying this display of one's social skills should be tidbits of comic business with jeweled fans or snuffboxes, coy glances and inviting winks, fluttering eyelashes and tilted heads, frivolous gestures and meaningless sighs—all helping to conceal or disguise the emptiness behind the smartly decorated mask.

In a comedy of manners what is *said* or what is *done* is not nearly as important as *how* it is revealed. The actor must be able to portray the nimbleness of wit and the attitude of carefree leisure that most accurately reflect the historical period.

Cast:

    Sir Peter
    Lady Teazle

Scene:

    A dressing room in Sir Peter Teazle's house, early morning.

ACT II, SCENE I

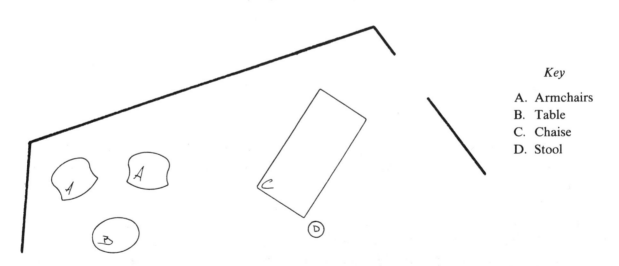

Key

A. Armchairs
B. Table
C. Chaise
D. Stool

Sir Peter Teazle, a middle-aged gentleman of a stubborn and quarrelsome nature, has recently married an innocent, and much younger, girl from the country. Although pleasant and gentle herself, Lady Teazle has become involved with a circle of vicious gossips and in trying to imitate their life-styles has become very lavish and careless in spending her husband's fortune.

Not without reason, Sir Peter is disturbed and has decided to confront his wife in her dressing room. The scene begins with considerable energy as Sir Peter paces back and forth like a caged lion while Lady Teazle, calm and reserved, rests precariously on a chaise. By the conclusion of the scene, however, the initial roles have been reversed and it is Lady Teazle who rushes off, leaving Sir Peter to reflect on what a lucky man he is to have such a charming wife.

[1] Paces.

[2] Fans herself.

[3] Sits on foot of the chaise, facing her.

[4] Jumps up and crosses down right.

[5] Sits upright with feet on the floor.

[6] Crosses to above the table, removes a flower from vase, and flings it down center.

[7] Retrieves the flower and sits on chair center, as she places it in a vase.

[8] Paces above the table.

[9] Sits next to her and removes the flower from the vase. He removes it several times until he holds it by the stem, and she by the bud.

[10] They break it.

SIR PETER: Lady Teazle, [1] Lady Teazle, I'll not bear it!

LADY TEAZLE: Sir Peter, [2] Sir Peter, you may bear it or not, as you please; but I ought to have my own way in everything, and what's more, I will, too. What! though I was educated in the country, I know very well that women of fashion in London are accountable to nobody after they are married.

SIR PETER: Very well, ma'am, very well—[3] so a husband is to have no influence, no authority?

LADY TEAZLE: Authority! No, to be sure: if you wanted authority over me, you should have adopted me, and not married me. I am sure you were old enough.

SIR PETER: Old enough! [4] Ay, there it is. Well, well, Lady Teazle, though my life may be made unhappy by your temper, I'll not be ruined by your extravagance.

LADY TEAZLE: My extravagance! [5] I'm sure I'm not more extravagant than a woman of fashion ought to be.

SIR PETER: No, [6] no, madam, you shall throw away no more sums on such unmeaning luxury. 'Slife! to spend as much to furnish your dressing room with flowers in winter as would suffice to turn the Pantheon into a greenhouse, and give a *fête champêtre* at Christmas.

LADY TEAZLE: And am I to blame, [7] Sir Peter, because flowers are dear in cold weather? You should find fault with the climate, and not with me. For my part, I'm sure, I wish it was spring all the year round, and that roses grew under one's feet!

SIR PETER: Oons! [8] madam—if you had been born to this, I shouldn't wonder at your talking thus; but you forget what your situation was when I married you.

LADY TEAZLE: No, no, I don't; 'twas a very disagreeable one, or I should never have married you.

SIR PETER: Yes, [9] yes, madam, you were then in somewhat a humbler style: the daughter of a plain country squire. Recollect, Lady Teazle, when I saw you first sitting at your tambour, in a pretty figured linen gown, with a bunch of keys at your side; your hair combed smooth over a roll, and your apartment hung round with fruits in worsted, of your own making.

LADY TEAZLE: O, [10] yes! I remember it very well, and a curious

[11] Twirls stem and then rises.

[12] Turns chair to face left and drops crushed bud into vase.

[13] Crosses down right and then to foot of chaise.

[14] Whirls to face her, and then sits on chaise.

[15] Rises and crosses above table to the chair right and sits, facing right.

[16] Rises and crosses above chaise to its head, and leans upon it.

[17] Glances over her shoulder at him.

[18] Rises.

[19] Slowly turns to face him.

[20] Crosses to the chaise and reclines upon it.

[21] Crosses to above chaise and then to stool, where he sits facing her.

[22] Attempting to touch her hand.

[23] She removes her hand from his reach and then fans herself.

[24] He rises and storms angrily down left.

[25] Grooms her coif.

life I led. My daily occupation to inspect the dairy, superintend the poultry, make extracts from the family receipt-book—and comb my aunt Deborah's lapdog.

SIR PETER: Yes, [11] yes, ma'am, 'twas so indeed.

LADY TEAZLE: And then, [12] you know, my evening amusements! To draw patterns for ruffles, which I had not materials to make up; to play Pope Joan with the curate; to read a sermon to my aunt; or to be stuck down to an old spinet to strum my father to sleep after a fox-chase.

SIR PETER: [13] I am glad you have so good a memory. Yes, madam, these were the recreations I took you from; but now you must have your coach—*vis-à-vis*—and three powdered footmen before your chair; and, in the summer, a pair of white cats to draw you to Kensington Gardens. No recollections, [14] I suppose, when you were content to ride double, behind the butler, on a dock'd coach-horse.

LADY TEAZLE: No—I swear I never did that: [15] I deny the butler and the coach-horse.

SIR PETER: This, [16] madam, was your situation; and what have I done for you? I have made you a woman of fashion, of fortune, of rank; in short, I have made you my wife.

LADY TEAZLE: Well, [17] then—and there is but one thing more you can make me to add to the obligation, and that is—.

SIR PETER: My widow, I suppose?

LADY TEAZLE: Hem! [18] hem!

SIR PETER: [19] I thank you madam—but don't flatter yourself; for though your ill conduct may disturb my peace, it shall never break my heart, I promise you: however, I am equally obliged to you for the hint.

LADY TEAZLE: [20] Then why will you endeavour to make yourself so disagreeable to me, and thwart me in every little elegant expense?

SIR PETER: 'Slife, [21] madam, I say, had you any of these little elegant expenses when you married me?

LADY TEAZLE: Lud, [22] Sir Peter! would you have me be out of the fashion?

SIR PETER: The fashion, [23] indeed! what had you to do with the fashion before you married me?

LADY TEAZLE: For my part, [24] I should think you would like to have your wife thought a woman of taste.

SIR PETER: Ay—there again—taste—. Zounds! madam, you had no taste when you married me!

LADY TEAZLE: That's very true indeed, [25] Sir Peter; and after

26 Crosses to down right.

27 Pulls hand mirror from under the chaise and then examines her makeup.

28 Performs chin exercises and then eye massages.

29 With her face manipulated into a horrible grimace.

30 Rushes to the foot of the chaise.

31 Rises and stands below head of the chaise.

32 Steps to him and takes his hand, as he avoids her gaze.

33 Turns to look at her.

34 Rushes off down left.

35 Follows her down left.

36 Crosses slowly to down right.

37 Crosses to chaise and lounges on it as the curtain falls.

having married you, I should never pretend to taste again, I allow. But now, Sir Peter, if we have finished our daily jangle, I presume I may go to my engagement at Lady Sneerwell's.

SIR PETER: Ay, 26 there's another precious circumstance. A charming set of acquaintance you have made there.

LADY TEAZLE: Nay, 27 Sir Peter, they are all people of rank and fortune, and remarkably tenacious of reputation.

SIR PETER: Yes, 28 egad, they are tenacious of reputation with a vengeance; for they don't choose anybody should have a character but themselves! Such a crew! Ah! many a wretch has rid on a hurdle who has done less mischief than these utterers of forged tales, coiners of scandal, and clippers of reputation.

LADY TEAZLE: What! 29 would you restrain the freedom of speech?

SIR PETER: Oh! 30 they have made you just as bad as any one of the society.

LADY TEAZLE: Why, 31 I believe I do bear a part with a tolerable grace. But I vow I bear no malice against the people I abuse. When I say an ill-natured thing, 'tis out of pure good humour; and I take it for granted, they deal exactly in the same manner with me. But, 32 Sir Peter, you know what you promised: to come to Lady Sneerwell's too.

SIR PETER: Well, 33 well, I'll call in just to look after my own character.

LADY TEAZLE: 34 Then indeed you must make haste after me, or you'll be too late. So goodbye to you.35

SIR PETER: So—I have gained much by my intended expostulation: yet, 36 with what a charming air she contradicts everything I say, and how pleasingly she shows her contempt for my authority! Well, though I can't make her love me, there is great satisfaction in quarrelling with her; 37 and I think she never appears to such advantage as when she is doing everything in her power to plague me.

Having fled her home several hours earlier, Lady Teazle pays a visit to the notorious Lady Sneerwell, who is presiding over an afternoon meeting of the society gossips. Here are gathered all the frivolous fops, would-be poets, biting wits, and pretentious matrons of the upper class.

The clan has gathered for chamber music, refreshments, and the anticipated daily report of Mrs. Candour, who delights in chronicling the current scandals and intrigues that are making the rounds of the city. Lady Teazle is at first an observer but soon joins the others to contribute a juicy, if not altogether untruthful, rumor that signals her acceptance into the group. The merriment of the occasion, however, is soon interrupted by Sir Peter, who has come to reclaim his wife and her precious reputation.

In playing the scene there should be a suggestion of polite chit-chat touched with bitter satire and a biting wit that helps to distinguish each of the social "types" who have gathered. There should also be an emphasis upon gross deceit and sharp ridicule, mirrored in the tone with which the dialogue is spoken.

Sir Peter's asides, spoken directly to the audience, should be crisp and conversational, to contrast with the more precise and rapierlike exchanges between the members of the school for scandal.

ACT II, Scene ii

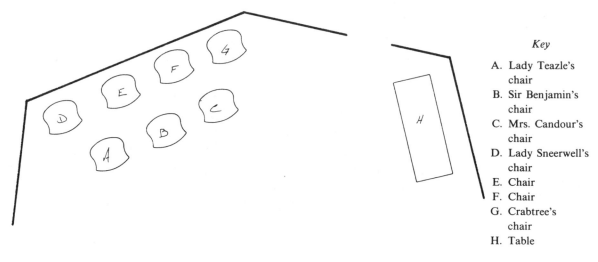

Key

A. Lady Teazle's chair
B. Sir Benjamin's chair
C. Mrs. Candour's chair
D. Lady Sneerwell's chair
E. Chair
F. Chair
G. Crabtree's chair
H. Table

Cast:

Lady Teazle	Sir Benjamin
Mrs. Candour	Sir Peter
Lady Sneerwell	Crabtree

Scene:

Lady Sneerwell's house, several hours later. A music room in midafternoon.

[1] Sotto voce from behind her fan.	**LADY TEAZLE:** [1] What's the matter, Mrs. Candour?
[2] Leans over Sir Benjamin.	**MRS. CANDOUR:** [2] They'll not allow our friend Miss Vermillion to be handsome.
[3] Leans forward.	**LADY SNEERWELL:** Oh, [3] surely she is a pretty woman.
[4] Stands.	**CRABTREE:** [4] I am very glad you think so, ma'am.[5]
[5] Bows and sits.	**MRS. CANDOUR:** [6] She has a charming fresh color.
[6] Smiles as she waves to some unseen guest.	**LADY TEAZLE:** Yes, when it is fresh put on.
[7] Turns to her.	**MRS. CANDOUR:** Oh, [7] fie! I'll swear her color is natural: I have seen it come and go!

[8] Sir Benjamin opens his eyes; he has not been asleep.

[9] Very loudly, until they quiet him.

[10] Stands.

[11] Bows and sits.

[12] Sir Benjamin beckons Crabtree forward, and Crabtree obliges by leaning across Mrs. Candour.

[13] Very loudly, as Crabtree withdraws to his chair with a hand to his now deafened ear.

[14] Turns slightly to Lady Sneerwell.

[15] Very loudly. They quiet him, and he finally speaks in a lower voice.

[16] Rapping Sir Benjamin with her fan.

[17] Switches seats with Sir Benjamin.

[18] Switches seats with Sir Benjamin.

[19] Enters up left and bows.

[20] Steps downstage.

LADY TEAZLE: I dare swear you have, ma'am: [8] it goes off at night and comes again in the morning.

SIR BENJAMIN: True, [9] ma'am, it not only comes and goes; but, what's more, egad, her maid can fetch and carry it!

MRS. CANDOUR: Ha! ha! ha! how I hate to hear you talk so! But surely, now, her sister is, or was, very handsome.

CRABTREE: Who? [10] Mrs. Evergreen? O Lord! she's six-and-fifty if she's an hour![11]

MRS. CANDOUR: How positively you wrong her; fifty-two or fifty-three is the utmost— [12] and I don't think she looks more.

SIR BENJAMIN: Ah! [13] there's no judging by her looks, unless one could see her face.

LADY SNEERWELL: Well, [14] well, if Mrs. Evergreen does take some pains to repair the ravages of time, you must allow she effects it with great ingenuity; and surely that's better than the careless manner in which the widow Ochre caulks her wrinkles.

SIR BENJAMIN: Nay, [15] now, Lady Sneerwell, you are severe upon the widow. Come, come, 'tis not that she paints so ill—but, when she has finished her face, she joins it on so badly to her neck, that she looks like a mended statue, in which the connoisseur may see at once that the head's modern, though the trunk's antique!

CRABTREE: Ha! ha! ha! Well said, nephew!

MRS. CANDOUR: Ha! ha! ha! [16] Well, you make me laugh; but I vow I hate you for it. What do you think of Miss Simper?

SIR BENJAMIN: Why, she has very pretty teeth.

LADY TEAZLE: Yes; and on that account, when she is neither speaking nor laughing (which very seldom happens), she never absolutely shuts her mouth, but leaves it always on ajar, as it were—thus.

MRS. CANDOUR: How can you be so ill-natured?

LADY TEAZLE: Nay, [17] I allow even that's better than the pains Mrs. Prim takes to conceal her losses in front. She draws her mouth till it positively resembles the aperture of a poor's box, and all her words appear to slide out edgewise, as it were—thus: *How do you do, madam? Yes, madam.*

LADY SNEERWELL: Very well, [18] Lady Teazle; I see you can be a little severe.

LADY TEAZLE: In defence of a friend it is but justice. But here comes Sir Peter to spoil our pleasantry.

SIR PETER: Ladies, [19] your most obedient. (Aside.) [20] Mercy on me, here is the whole set! A character dead at every word, I suppose.

[21] Crabtree rises to allow Sir Peter to enter the aisle.

[22] Enters aisle to chair F but does not sit. He stands to observe the group.

[23] Crabtree resumes his seat with a little bow, which all ignore.

[24] Switches seats with Lady Sneerwell in order to speak directly to Sir Benjamin.

[25] They all turn to stare at him. A pause. He sits, and they resume.

[26] Slides his chair up to the left of Mrs. Candour.

[27] Rushes to table for sweets. Fills her handkerchief with several and returns to her seat.

[28] All except Sir Peter reach into Mrs. Candour's lap for a sweet.

[29] Reaches into her lap for a sweet, and sadly discovers that the handkerchief is empty.

[30] Slides his chair up to the right of Lady Teazle.

[31] Rises.

[32] They all ignore him.

[33] Still standing.

[34] Looks up at Sir Peter.

MRS. CANDOUR: [21] I am rejoiced you are come, Sir Peter. They have been so censorious—and Lady Teazle as bad as any one.

SIR PETER: That must be very distressing to you, [22] Mrs. Candour, I dare swear.

MRS. CANDOUR: Oh, [23] they will allow good qualities to nobody; not even good nature to our friend Mrs. Pursy.

LADY TEAZLE: What, the fat dowager who was at Mrs. Quadrille's last night.

MRS. CANDOUR: Nay, her bulk is her misfortune; and when she takes so much pains to get rid of it, you ought not to reflect on her.

LADY SNEERWELL: That's very true, indeed.

LADY TEAZLE: Yes, [24] I know she almost lives on acids and small whey; laces herself by pulleys; and often, in the hottest noon in summer, you may see her on a little squat pony, with her hair plaited up behind like a drummer's and puffing round the ring on a full trot.

MRS. CANDOUR: I thank you, Lady Teazle, for defending her.

SIR PETER: Yes, [25] a good defence, truly.

MRS. CANDOUR: Truly, Lady Teazle is as censorious as Miss Sallow.

CRABTREE: Yes, [26] and she is a curious being to pretend to be censorious—an awkward gawky, without any one good point under heaven.

MRS. CANDOUR: [27] Positively you shall not be so very severe. Miss Sallow is a near relation of mine by marriage, and, as for her person, great allowance is to be made; for, let me tell you, a woman labors under many disadvantages who tries to pass for a girl of six-and-thirty.

LADY SNEERWELL: Though, [28] surely, she is handsome still— and for the weakness in her eyes, considering how much she reads by candlelight, it is not to be wondered at.

MRS. CANDOUR: True; [29] and then as to her manner, upon my word, I think it is particularly graceful, considering she never had the least education; for you know her mother was a Welsh milliner, and her father a sugar-baker at Bristol.

SIR BENJAMIN: Ah! [30] you are both of you too good-natured!

SIR PETER: (Aside.) Yes, [31] damned good-natured! This their own relation! mercy on me!

MRS. CANDOUR: For my part, [32] I own I cannot bear to hear a friend ill spoken of.

SIR PETER: No, [33] to be sure.

SIR BENJAMIN: Oh! [34] you are of a moral turn. Mrs. Candour

35 Crosses to the table for another helping of sweets, and then returns to her seat.

36 Passes a sweet from Mrs. Candour to Lady Sneerwell, who passes it to Lady Teazle, who passes it to Sir Benjamin, who eats it.

37 The passing is repeated, but Lady Teazle eats the sweet while Sir Benjamin looks disappointed.

38 The passing is repeated, but Lady Sneerwell eats the sweet while Lady Teazle looks disappointed.

39 Pops a sweet into the mouth of Mrs. Candour while Lady Sneerwell looks disappointed.

40 Crabtree pops a sweet into his own mouth as Lady Teazle and Mrs. Candour both look disappointed.

41 Still standing and observing.

42 She notices her empty handkerchief and puts it away.

43 The music stops. All but Sir Peter applaud politely. He crosses to down left of center.

44 The applause stops. She crosses down to Sir Peter.

45 Crosses to right of her.

46 Crosses down to his right.

47 Crosses down to right of her.

48 Crosses to the table to pour wine for all.

and I can sit for an hour and hear Lady Stucco talk sentiment.

LADY TEAZLE: Nay, I vow Lady Stucco is very well with the dessert after dinner; for she's just like the French fruit one cracks for mottoes—made up of paint and proverb.

MRS. CANDOUR: Well, 35 I will never join in ridiculing a friend; and so I constantly tell my cousin Ogle, and you all know what pretensions she has to be critical on beauty.

CRABTREE: Oh, 36 to be sure! she has herself the oddest countenance that ever was seen; 'tis a collection of features from all the different countries of the globe.

SIR BENJAMIN: So she has, indeed—an Irish front—.

CRABTREE: 37 Caledonian locks—.

SIR BENJAMIN: Dutch nose—.

CRABTREE: Austrian lips—.

SIR BENJAMIN: 38 Complexion of a Spaniard—.

CRABTREE: And teeth *à la Chinoise*—.

SIR BENJAMIN: In short, her face resembles a *table d' hôte* at Spa—where no two guests are of a nation—.

CRABTREE: 39 Or a congress at the close of a general war—wherein all the members, even to her eyes, appear to have a different interest, and her nose and chin are the only parties likely to join issue.

MRS. CANDOUR: Ha! ha! ha!40

SIR PETER: (Aside.) 41 Mercy on my life!—a person they dine with twice a week!

LADY SNEERWELL: Go—go—you are a couple of provoking toads.

MRS. CANDOUR: Nay, 42 but I vow you shall not carry the laugh off so—for give me leave to say, that Mrs. Ogle—.

SIR PETER: Madam, 43 madam, I beg your pardon—there's no stopping these good gentlemen's tongues. But when I tell you, Mrs. Candour, that the lady they are abusing is a particular friend of mine, I hope you'll not take her part.

LADY SNEERWELL: 44 Ha! ha! ha! well said, Sir Peter! but you are a cruel creature—too phlegmatic for a jest yourself, and too peevish to allow wit in others.

SIR PETER: Ah, 45 madam, true wit is more nearly allied to good nature than your ladyship is aware of.

LADY TEAZLE: True, 46 Sir Peter: I believe they are so near akin that they can never be united.

SIR BENJAMIN: Or rather, 47 madam, I suppose them man and wife because one seldom sees them together.

LADY TEAZLE: 48 But Sir Peter is such an enemy to scandal, I

[49] Lady Sneerwell crosses to the table and takes a full glass. She gives it to Crabtree and takes another.

[50] Crosses to Sir Peter and hands him the glass of wine. He returns it to the table.

[51] Hands Mrs. Candour a glass of wine and crosses to down right.

[52] Almost chokes on her wine.

[53] Crosses to down right.

[54] Crosses to up left.

[55] Crosses to down right.

[56] Lady Teazle crosses to down right and brings a glass of wine for Sir Benjamin.

[57] Bows and then exits up left.

[58] Rises and crosses to down center.

[59] They all laugh, and exit down right.

believe he would have it put down by Parliament.

SIR PETER: 'Fore heaven, [49] madam, if they were to consider the sporting with reputation of as much importance as poaching on manors, and pass an act for the preservation of fame, I believe many would thank them for the bill.

LADY SNEERWELL: O Lud! Sir Peter, [50] would you deprive us of our privileges?

SIR PETER: Ay, [51] madam; and then no person should be permitted to kill characters and run down reputations, but qualified old maids and disappointed widows.

LADY SNEERWELL: Go, [52] you monster!

MRS. CANDOUR: But, [53] surely, you would not be quite so severe on those who only report what they hear?

SIR PETER: Yes, madam, I would have law merchant for them too; and in all cases of slander currency, whenever the drawer of the lie was not to be found, [54] the injured parties should have a right to come on any of the indorsers.

CRABTREE: Well, [55] for my part, I believe there never was a scandalous tale without some foundation.

LADY SNEERWELL: Come, [56] ladies, shall we sit down to cards in the next room? Sir Peter, you are not going to leave us?

SIR PETER: Your ladyship must excuse me: I'm called away by particular business. But I leave my character behind me.[57]

SIR BENJAMIN: Well—certainly, [58] Lady Teazle, that lord of yours is a strange being. I could tell you some stories of him would make you laugh heartily if he were not your husband.

LADY TEAZLE: Oh, pray don't mind that; come, do let's hear them.[59]

FROM

Fashion (1845)
by ANNA CORA MOWATT

Mr. Tiffany's success as a merchant leads his vain wife to assume the affectations and presumptions of high society and literally to open her doors to all the presumed poets, artists, and exiled nobles of the day. Trueman, an honest but dull farmer and family friend, comes to visit his wealthy old neighbors and is dismayed to discover the superficiality and artifice that have invaded the Tiffany household.

With the aid of the virtuous Gertrude, the family governess, Trueman helps to awaken the Tiffanys to the deceit and trickery of the parasites, especially the scheming Court Jolimaitre, and leads them back to the virtues of the simple life, proving in his native wisdom the basic goodness and honesty of "Yankee ingenuity."

Fashion

As America's contribution to the comedy of manners style of playwriting, the script is intended as a good-natured satire upon the follies and affectations that often arise when a new nation begins to imitate foreign dress and speech. There is also the unabashed provincial pride expressed for the plain but inherently pure-of-heart American heroes who refused to adopt foreign fashions and manners.

Most of the social criticism expressed in the play concerns the awkwardness with which New York society tries to imitate continental taste and the fraud that foreign posturing perpetrates when it begins to replace native manners and customs.

In playing the scene the actor should keep in mind all of the general principles previously noted for the comedy of manners and slightly exaggerate both movement and voice to suggest that these characters are merely masquerading as sophisticated and refined members of high society.

There should be occasional mispronunciation of French phrases, awkward posture and painful posing, improper etiquette, and an uncomfortable appearance. The actor should also assume a boisterous laugh, frigid smile, and stiff posture to suggest that the impersonation is not a confident one. Fans, handkerchiefs, snuffboxes, and eyeglasses may also be used to punctuate exchanges of dialogue, but they should be handled incorrectly to highlight the inexperience of the character using them.

Cast:

Tiffany
Mrs. Tiffany
Count
Seraphina

Scene:

Mrs. Tiffany's parlor, late afternoon.

ACT III, Scene i

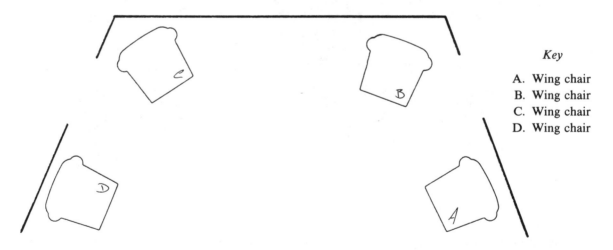

Key

A. Wing chair
B. Wing chair
C. Wing chair
D. Wing chair

As the scene opens, Mr. Tiffany is scolding his wife for her recent extravagance, and she is reprimanding him for clinging to outdated manners and customs now that they are a family of wealth. Although the exchange is civil for the most part, there is an undertone of anger and hostility that is only prevented from surfacing by the unexpected arrival of the dashing Count.

The humor of the scene lies in the polite games the characters play as they try to convince one another of their grace and sophistication. The reality of the situation, however, is that the Count is a disguised chef seeking a fortune by proposing to Seraphina, the Tiffanys' beautiful but naive daughter, and that the elder Tiffanys are so concerned with assuming proper social manners that they cannot see the truth of the matter.

[1] Rises and slowly crosses to chair, center. He whirls and sits so she cannot see him.

[2] Storms down left.

[3] Rises to speak.

[4] Sits in chair D.

[5] Crosses to above chair A.

[6] Hits chair A with his cane.

[7] Steps and hits chair B.

[8] Steps and hits chair C.

[9] Steps and hits chair B.

[10] Steps and hits chair A.

[11] Steps and hits chair B.

[12] Steps and hits chair C.

[13] Rises and paces from down right to up right, and then returns down right, where she watches Mr. Tiffany out of the corner of her eye.

[14] Crosses to down left and begins to pace from down left to down right.

[15] They almost collide. Adjusting, they continue to pace.

[16] Begins to pace, from up right to up left. They are headed in opposite directions at all times.

[17] The rate of the pacing begins to increase.

[18] They pace a bit faster.

[19] They pace a bit faster.

[20] They pace a bit faster.

TIFFANY: Your extravagance will ruin me, Mrs. Tiffany!

MRS. TIFFANY: [1] And your stinginess will ruin me, Mr. Tiffany! It is totally and *toot a fate* impossible to convince you of the necessity of *keeping up appearances*. There is a certain display which every woman of fashion is forced to make!

TIFFANY: [2] And pray who made *you* a woman of fashion?

MRS. TIFFANY: [3] What a vulgar question! All women of fashion, Mr. Tiffany—[4].

TIFFANY: [5] In this land are *self-constituted*, like you, Madam— [6] and *fashion* is the cloak for more sins than charity ever covered! [7] It was for *fashion's* sake that you insisted upon my purchasing this expensive house—[8] it was for *fashion's* sake that you ran me in debt at every exorbitant upholsterer's and extravagant furniture warehouse in the city—[9] it was for *fashion's* sake that you built that ruinous conservatory—[10] hired more servants than they have persons to wait upon—[11] and dressed your footman like a harlequin![12]

MRS. TIFFANY: Mr. Tiffany, [13] you are thoroughly plebeian and insufferably *American* in your grovelling ideas. And, pray, what was the occasion of these very *mal-ap-pro-pos* remarks? Merely because I requested a paltry fifty dollars to purchase a new style of head-dress—a *bijou* of an article just introduced in France.

TIFFANY: Time was, [14] Mrs. Tiffany, when you manufactured your own French head-dresses—then sold them to your shortest-sighted customers. And all you knew about France, or French either, was what you spelt out at the bottom of your fashion-plates—but now you have grown so fashionable, [15] forsooth, that you have forgotten how to speak your mother tongue.

MRS. TIFFANY: Mr. Tiffany, [16] Mr. Tiffany! Nothing is more positively vulgarian—more *unaristocratic* than any allusion to the past!

TIFFANY: Why, [17] I thought, my dear, that *aristocrats* lived principally upon the past—and traded in the market of fashion with the bones of their ancestors for capital!

MRS. TIFFANY: Mr. Tiffany, [18] such vulgar remarks are only suitable to the counting-house; in my drawing room you should—.

TIFFANY: [19] Vary my sentiments with my locality, as you change your *manners* with your *dress!*

MRS. TIFFANY: Mr. Tiffany, [20] I desire that you will purchase

²¹ They suddenly freeze. He is down right, and she is up left.

²² They very slowly begin to pace again, she from up left to down left, and he from down right to up right.

²³ Once again, the pacing picks up in tempo.

²⁴ They pace a bit faster.

²⁵ They suddenly freeze. He is up right, and she is down left.

²⁶ He crosses to chair D and sits.

²⁷ She crosses to chair A and sits.

²⁸ Rises.

²⁹ Crosses to her.

³⁰ Falls into chair B.

³¹ Rises.

³² Crosses to chair C.

Count d'Orsay's "Science of Etiquette," and learn how to conduct yourself—especially before you appear at the grand ball—which I shall give on Friday!

TIFFANY: Confound your balls, Madam; ²¹ they make *footballs* of my money, while you dance away all that I am worth! A pretty time to give a ball when you know that I am on the very brink of bankruptcy!

MRS. TIFFANY: So much the greater reason that nobody should suspect your circumstances, or you would lose your credit at once. Just at this crisis a ball is absolutely *necessary* to save your reputation. ²² There is Mrs. Adolphus Dashaway—she gave the most splendid *fete* of the season—and I hear on very good authority that her husband has not paid his baker's bill in three months. Then there was Mrs. Honeywood—.

TIFFANY: Gave a ball the night before her husband shot himself—. ²³ Perhaps you wish to drive me to follow his example?

MRS. TIFFANY: Good gracious! Mr. Tiffany, how you talk. I beg you won't mention anything of the kind. I consider black the most unbecoming color. I'm sure I've done all that I could to gratify you. ²⁴ There is that vulgar old torment, Trueman, who gives one the lie fifty times a day—haven't I been very civil to him?

TIFFANY: Civil to his *wealth*, Mrs. Tiffany! ²⁵ I told you that he was a rich old farmer—the early friend of my father—my own benefactor—and that I had reason to think he might assist me in my present embarrassments. Your civility was *bought*—and like most of your *own* purchases ²⁶ has yet to be *paid* for.

MRS. TIFFANY: And will be, no doubt! ²⁷ The condescension of a woman of fashion should command any price. Mr. Trueman is insupportably indecorous—he has insulted Count Jolimaitre in the most outrageous manner. If the Count was not so deeply interested—so *abime* with Seraphina, I am sure he would never honour us by his visits again!

TIFFANY: So much the better—²⁸ he shall never marry my daughter! I am resolved on that. Why, madam, I am told there is in Paris a regular matrimonial stock company, who fit out indigent dandies for the market. ²⁹ How do I know but this fellow is one of its creatures, and that he has come here to increase its dividends by marrying a fortune?³⁰

MRS. TIFFANY: Nonsense, Mr. Tiffany. ³¹ The Count, the most fashionable young man in all New York—the intimate friend of all the dukes and lords in Europe—³² not marry my daughter?

[33] Sits.

[34] The Count enters up left.

[35] The Count clears his throat.

[36] Extends her hand.

[37] The Count moves to her, bows, and kisses her hand.

[38] Seraphina enters up right.

[39] Crosses to chair D. The Count bows and kisses her hand, and she sits.

[40] The Count bows and extends his hand. Mr. Tiffany folds his arms. There is an awkward and tense pause.

[41] Crosses to chair A and sits.

[42] Rises.

[43] Rises.

[44] Rises.

[45] They sit. There is another awkward and tense pause, as Mrs. Tiffany moves up right.

[46] Despite her gestures, he does not move.

[47] Crosses behind him, grabs his ear and leads him off right.

[48] Crosses behind Seraphina, who moves to chair C.

[49] Moves behind Seraphina, who crosses to chair B.

[50] Crosses behind Seraphina, who moves to chair A.

[51] Moves behind Seraphina, who sits.

[52] Rises, takes his arm, and leads him down left.

Not permit my Seraphina to become a Countess? Mr. Tiffany, [33] you are out of your senses!

TIFFANY: [34] That would not be very wonderful, considering how many years I have been united to you, my dear. Modern physicians pronounce lunacy infectious![35]

MRS. TIFFANY: My dear Count, [36] I am overjoyed at the very sight of you.

COUNT: [37] Flattered myself you'd be glad to see me, Madam— knew it was not your *jour de reception.*

MRS. TIFFANY: But for you, Count, all days—

COUNT: I thought so. [38] Ah, Miss Tiffany, on my honour, you're looking beautiful.

SERAPHINA: Count, [39] flattery from you—

COUNT: Your worthy Papa, I believe? Sir, [40] your most obedient.

MRS. TIFFANY: I hope that we shall have the pleasure of seeing you on Friday evening, Count?

COUNT: [41] Madam, my invitations—my engagements—so numerous—I can hardly answer for myself: and you Americans take offense so easily.

MRS. TIFFANY: But, [42] Count, everybody expects you at our ball— you are the principal attraction.

SERAPHINA: Count, [43] you *must* come!

COUNT: [44] Since you insist—aw—aw—there's no resisting you, Miss Tiffany.

SERAPHINA: I am so thankful. [45] How can I repay your condescension?

MRS. TIFFANY: Mr. Tiffany, pray come here—I have something particular to say.

TIFFANY: Then speak out, [46] my dear. I thought it was highly improper just now to leave a girl with a young man?

MRS. TIFFANY: Oh, [47] but the Count that is difficult!

TIFFANY: I suppose you mean to say there's nothing of *the man* about him?

COUNT: (Aside.) Not a moment to lose! (To her.) Miss Tiffany, [48] I have an unpleasant—a particularly unpleasant piece of intelligence. You see, [49] I have just received a letter from my friend the—aw—[50] the Earl of Airshire. The truth is, the Earl's daughter—beg you won't mention it—[51] has distinguished me by a tender *penchant.*

SERAPHINA: I understand. [52] And they wish you to return and marry the young lady. But surely you will not leave us, Count?

COUNT: If *you* bid me stay—I shouldn't have the conscience—I

[53] Crosses to down center.

[54] Crosses to him and takes his arm.

[55] Crosses to down right.

[56] Crosses to him and takes his arm.

[57] Crosses to down center.

[58] Crosses back to Seraphina.

[59] Escorts her to down center.

[60] Crosses down left.

[61] Crosses to her and takes her in his arms.

[62] A pause. They lean their heads together and smile. Just as their lips are about to meet in a tender kiss,

[63] Mrs. Tiffany enters from up right and crosses to up center.

[64] Crosses to her and bows.

[65] Bows and exits up left in a hurry.

[66] Grabs Seraphina's arm and leads her off, up right.

couldn't *afford* to tear myself away. (Aside.) I'm sure that's honest.[53]

SERAPHINA: Oh, [54] Count!

COUNT: Say but one word—[55] say that you shouldn't mind being made a Countess—and I'll break with the Earl tomorrow.

SERAPHINA: Count, [56] this surprises—but don't think of leaving the country! We could not pass the time without you! I—yes, yes, Count! I do consent!

COUNT: (Aside.) [57] I thought she would! (To her.) Enchanted, [58] rapture, bliss, ecstasy, and all that sort of thing. Words can't express it, but you understand. But it must be kept a secret—positively it *must*. [59] If the rumour of our engagement were whispered abroad—the Earl's daughter—the delicacy of my situation—aw—you comprehend? It is even possible that our nuptials, my charming Miss Tiffany, *our nuptials* must take place in private!

SERAPHINA: Oh, [60] that is quite impossible!

COUNT: It's the latest fashion abroad. [61] The very latest! Ah, I knew that would determine you. Can I depend on your secrecy?[62]

SERAPHINA: Oh, yes! Believe me!

MRS. TIFFANY: [63] The brand new carriage is below! Count, my daughter and I are about to take an airing in our new *voyture*—will you honour us with your company?

COUNT: I—[64] I have a most *pressing* engagement. A letter to write to the Earl of Airshire—who is at present residing in—aw—the Isle of Skye. I must bid you good morning.[65]

MRS. TIFFANY: Good morning, Count. Come, [66] Seraphina. Come!

FROM

The Importance of Being Earnest (1895)
by OSCAR WILDE

At first glance, this "trivial play for serious people" seems a cobweb of deception, misunderstanding, and mistaken identity. Beginning with a series of episodes in which two young sophisticates seek the hands of two young and reserved ladies, the play suddenly shifts focus to reveal the more serious nature of extravagantly absurd and artificial customs and attitudes that govern polite society.

The characters are not realistic, and the obstacles they face before eventual reunion are not without moments of intrigue and amusing invention. In their witty exchanges they are always charming and elegant, even when saying disagreeable things. They follow a definite pattern of behavior accepted in the historical time as the "proper" way to live in a civilized society, and any departure from it would be considered "barbaric."

The Importance of Being Earnest

It is typical of this comedy of manners that the humor arises from the sparkling dialogue, the social amenities, and the always charming precision with which etiquette and high fashion are displayed. All young men are would-be wits and all young ladies are exquisite hostesses.

In playing the scene the actor should be aware that it is traditionally "presentational," or audience-centered, style, and no attempt is made to disguise the fact that this is a theatrical performance. The actor should face the audience as often as possible and speak in a clear and precise voice. Every movement, stance, and pose should be elegant and poised, and exchanges of dialogue should be punctuated with the use of fans or handkerchiefs.

Although there is no need to appear artificial or stiff, there should be a suggestion of erect posture and studied gesture to lend historical authenticity to the superficial type of characters. There should also be a suggestion of overly polite manners and delicacy of behavior in the relationship between the young man and the young lady.

Cast:

    Jack

    Gwendolen

    Lady Bracknell

Scene:

    Morning room in Algernon's flat in Half-Moon Street. The room is luxuriously and artistically furnished. The sound of a piano can be heard in the adjoining room.

ACT I

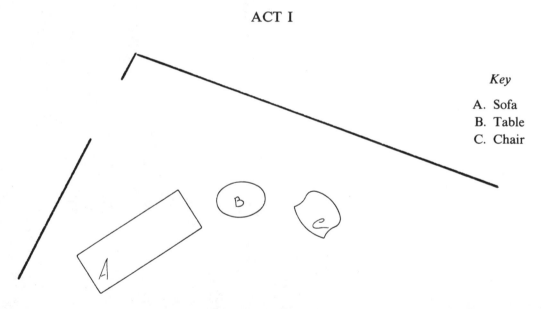

Key

A. Sofa
B. Table
C. Chair

Jack, a rascal and spendthrift, finds himself hopelessly in love at first sight with Gwendolen, a refined and attractive young lady who fancies herself the most precious and desirable beauty in society. He secretly wishes for an opportunity to be alone with her so that he may reveal his feelings; and the moment is provided when Lady Bracknell, Gwendolen's prudish and snappish mother, unexpectedly retires from the room to listen to a program of chamber music prepared by Jack's best friend, Algernon.

As the scene opens, there is an uncomfortable moment of silence, with Gwendolen seated nervously on the sofa and Jack standing shyly near the upstage chair. He is concerned that his reputation as an extravagant and carefree gentleman will not appeal to such a charming lady; and she is concerned that the man for whom she feels such a strong attraction may not propose in the romantic manner she hopes for.

[1] Clearing his throat.

[2] Rises and crosses down left, with her back to him.

[3] Rushes to sofa.

[4] Crosses down right center.

[5] Crosses to her.

[6] Turns to face him, and then turns away.

[7] He tries to touch her shoulder, nervously.

[8] She turns to face him.

[9] He presses her gloved hand to his cheek.

[10] She suddenly crosses down left, as he follows.

[11] She suddenly crosses down right, as he follows.

[12] She stops abruptly.

[13] Turns to him, with eyes closed and arms extended.

[14] He is frozen.

[15] Opening her eyes and moving her arms to emphasize expectation of an embrace.

[16] Crosses to chair, with back to her.

[17] Turns to her.

[18] Crosses to the sofa and sits.

[19] Rushes to the sofa and sits next to her.

JACK: [1] Charming day it has been, Miss Fairfax.

GWENDOLEN: [2] Pray don't talk to me about the weather, Mr. Worthing. Whenever people talk to me about the weather, I always feel quite certain that they mean something else. And that makes me so nervous.

JACK: I do mean something else.[3]

GWENDOLEN: I thought so. [4] In fact, I am never wrong.

JACK: [5] And I would like to be allowed to take advantage of Lady Bracknell's temporary absence . . .

GWENDOLEN: [6] I would certainly advise you to do so. Mamma has a way of coming back suddenly into a room that I have often had to speak to her about.

JACK: Miss Fairfax, [7] ever since I met you I have admired you more than any girl . . . I have ever met since . . . I met you.

GWENDOLEN: Yes, [8] I am quite well aware of the fact. And I often wish that in public, at any rate, you had been more demonstrative. For me you have always had an irresistible fascination. [9] Even before I met you I was far from indifferent to you. [10] We live, as I hope you know, Mr. Worthing, in an age of ideals. The fact is constantly mentioned in the more expensive monthly magazines, [11] and has reached the provincial pulpits, I am told; and my ideal has always been to love someone of the name of [12] Ernest. There is something in that name that inspires confidence. [13] The moment Algernon first mentioned to me that he had a friend called Ernest, I knew I was destined to love you.

JACK: You really love me, [14] Gwendolen?

GWENDOLEN: Passionately!

JACK: Darling! You don't know how happy you've made me.

GWENDOLEN: My own Ernest![15]

JACK: [16] But you don't really mean to say that you couldn't love me if my name wasn't Ernest?

GWENDOLEN: But your name is Ernest.

JACK: Yes, [17] I know it is. But supposing it was something else? Do you mean to say you couldn't love me then?

GWENDOLEN: Ah! [18] that is clearly a metaphysical speculation, and like most metaphysical speculations has very little reference at all to the actual facts of real life, as we know them.

JACK: Personally, [19] darling, to speak quite candidly, I don't much

[20] Rises and moves to behind chair.

[21] Rises.

[22] Sits.

[23] Rises.

[24] Sits.

[25] Rises, and then crosses to chair.

[26] Sits in chair.

[27] Moves to her.

[28] Rises.

[29] Crosses down left.

[30] Turns to her.

[31] Rises and crosses to sofa to sit.

[32] Rushes to her.

[33] Stops him with her parasol.

[34] Tosses a pillow on the floor.

[35] Kneeling on the pillow.

[36] Places her parasol on the sofa and rises to embrace him as both collapse on the pillow.

care about the name of Ernest . . . I don't think the name suits me at all.

GWENDOLEN: It suits you perfectly. It is a divine name. It has a music of its own. It produces vibrations.

JACK: Well, [20] really, Gwendolen, I must say that I think there are lots of other much nicer names. I think Jack, for instance, a charming name.

GWENDOLEN: Jack? [21] No, there is very little music in the name Jack, if any at all, indeed. [22] It does not thrill. [23] It produces absolutely no vibrations. [24] I have known several Jacks, and they all, without exception, were more than usually plain. [25] Besides, Jack is a notorious domesticity for John! And I pity any woman who is married to a man called John. She would probably never be allowed to know the entrancing pleasure of a single moment's solitude. The only really safe name is Ernest.[26]

JACK: Gwendolen, [27] I must get christened at once—I mean we must get married at once. There is no time to be lost.

GWENDOLEN: Married, [28] Mr. Worthing?

JACK: Well, [29] surely. You know that I love you, and you led me to believe, Miss Fairfax, that you were not absolutely indifferent to me.

GWENDOLEN: I adore you. But you haven't proposed to me yet. Nothing has been said at all about marriage. The subject has not even been touched on.

JACK: Well, [30] may I propose to you now?

GWENDOLEN: [31] I think it would be an admirable opportunity. And to spare you any possible disappointment, Mr. Worthing, I think it only fair to tell you quite frankly beforehand that I am fully determined to accept you.

JACK: Gwendolen![32]

GWENDOLEN: Yes, [33] Mr. Worthing, what have you got to say to me?

JACK: You know what I have got to say to you.

GWENDOLEN: Yes, [34] but you don't say it.

JACK: Gwendolen, [35] will you marry me?

GWENDOLEN: Of course I will, [36] darling. How long you have been about it! I am afraid you have had very little experience in how to propose.

JACK: My own one, I have never loved anyone in the world but you.

GWENDOLEN: Yes, but men often propose for practice. I know my brother Gerald does. All my girlfriends tell me so. What

[37] Enters from up left and stops abruptly.

[38] Rises and helps Jack to his feet.

[39] Crosses to chair and sits.

[40] Rises and crosses to center.

[41] Crosses to chair and sits.

[42] Crosses to her.

[43] Rises.

[44] Exits up right.

[45] Sits.

[46] Removes a notebook and pen from her purse and makes notations throughout the interview.

[47] Kicks the pillow under the sofa.

[48] Strolls casually down right to catch a glimpse of Gwendolen's carriage.

[49] Crosses to the sofa to retrieve the pillow. He is on his hands and knees as Lady Bracknell concludes her speech.

wonderfully blue eyes you have, Ernest! They are quite, quite blue. I hope you will always look at me just like that, especially when there are other people present.

LADY BRACKNELL: Mr. Worthing! Rise, [37] sir, from that semirecumbent posture. It is most indecorous.

GWENDOLEN: Mamma! [38] I must beg you to retire. This is no place for you. Besides, Mr. Worthing has not quite finished yet.

LADY BRACKNELL: Finished what, [39] may I ask?

GWENDOLEN: I am engaged to Mr. Worthing, mamma.

LADY BRACKNELL: Pardon me, [40] you are not engaged to anyone. When you do become engaged to someone, I, or your father, should his health permit him, will inform you of the fact. An engagement should come on a young girl as a surprise, pleasant or unpleasant, as the case may be. It is hardly a matter that she should be allowed to arrange for herself. [41] And now I have a few questions to put to you, Mr. Worthing. While I am making these inquiries, you, Gwendolen, will wait for me below in the carriage.

GWENDOLEN: Mamma![42]

LADY BRACKNELL: In the carriage, [43] Gwendolen! Gwendolen, the carriage!

GWENDOLEN: Yes, [44] mamma.

LADY BRACKNELL: You can take a seat, [45] Mr. Worthing.

JACK: Thank you, Lady Bracknell, I prefer standing.

LADY BRACKNELL: [46] I feel bound to tell you that you are not down on my list of eligible young men, although I have the same list as the dear Duchess of Bolton has. We work together, in fact. However, I am quite ready to enter your name, should your answers be what a really affectionate mother requires. Do you smoke?

JACK: Well, [47] yes, I must admit I smoke.

LADY BRACKNELL: I am glad to hear it. A man should always have an occupation of some kind. There are far too many idle men in London as it is. How old are you?

JACK: Twenty-nine.[48]

LADY BRACKNELL: A very good age to be married at. I have always been of the opinion that a man who desires to get married should know either everything or nothing. Which do you know?

JACK: I know nothing, [49] Lady Bracknell.

LADY BRACKNELL: I am pleased to hear it. I do not approve of anything that tampers with natural ignorance. Ignorance is

⁵⁰ Rises and examines his pocket watch, stopping abruptly as Lady Bracknell notes it in her book.

⁵¹ Crosses to the table and picks up a teacup and saucer.

⁵² His hands tremble, and he almost drops the cup and saucer.

⁵³ Places cup and saucer on the table.

⁵⁴ Overcome by a sneeze, he reaches into his pocket for a handkerchief.

⁵⁵ Replaces handkerchief and moves to the table for a bread-and-butter sandwich.

⁵⁶ Swallowing the sandwich and then choking.

⁵⁷ Bows head and folds hands.

like a delicate exotic fruit; touch it and the bloom is gone. The whole theory of modern education is radically unsound. Fortunately in England, at any rate, education produces no effect whatsoever. If it did, it would prove a serious danger to the upper classes, and probably lead to acts of violence in Grosvenor Square. What is your income?

JACK: ⁵⁰ Between seven and eight thousand a year.

LADY BRACKNELL: In land, or in investments?

JACK: In investments, chiefly.

LADY BRACKNELL: That is satisfactory. What between the duties expected of one during one's lifetime, and the duties exacted from one after one's death, land has ceased to be either a profit or a pleasure. It gives one position, and prevents one from keeping it up. That's all that can be said about land.

JACK: ⁵¹ I have a country house with some land, of course, attached to it, about fifteen hundred acres, I believe; but I don't depend on that for my real income. In fact, as far as I can make out, the poachers are the only people who make anything out of it.

LADY BRACKNELL: A country house! ⁵² How many bedrooms? Well, that point can be cleared up afterwards. You have a town house, I hope? A girl with a simple, unspoiled nature, like Gwendolen, could hardly be expected to reside in the country.

JACK: Well, ⁵³ I own a house in Belgrave Square, but it is let by the year to Lady Bloxham. Of course, I can get it back whenever I like, at six months' notice.

LADY BRACKNELL: Lady Bloxham? I don't know her.

JACK: Oh, ⁵⁴ she goes about very little. She is a lady considerably advanced in years.

LADY BRACKNELL: Ah, nowadays that is no guarantee of respectability of character. What number in Belgrave Square?

JACK: 149.

LADY BRACKNELL: The unfashionable side. I thought there was something. However, that could easily be altered.

JACK: ⁵⁵ Do you mean the fashion, or the side?

LADY BRACKNELL: Both, if necessary, I presume. What are your politics?

JACK: Well, ⁵⁶ I am afraid I really have none. I am a Liberal Unionist.

LADY BRACKNELL: Oh, they count as Tories. They dine with us. Or come in the evening, at any rate. Now to minor matters. Are your parents living?

JACK: ⁵⁷ I have lost both my parents.

58 Crosses to sofa.

59 Sits.

60 Rises.

61 Rises as Lady Bracknell sits.

62 Sits.

63 Rises.

64 Rises again as Lady Bracknell sits.

65 Crosses down right.

66 Rises.

67 Turns to face her.

68 Crosses center slowly as she closes the notebook and prepares to exit.

69 Crosses to her.

LADY BRACKNELL: To lose one parent, Mr. Worthing, may be regarded as a misfortune; to lose both looks like carelessness. Who was your father? He was evidently a man of some wealth. Was he born in what the Radical papers call the purple of commerce, or did he rise from the ranks of the aristocracy?

JACK: [58] I am afraid I really don't know. The fact is, Lady Bracknell, I said I had lost my parents. It would be nearer to the truth to say that my parents seem to have lost me. I don't actually know who I am by birth. I was . . . well, I was found.[59]

LADY BRACKNELL: Found![60]

JACK: [61] The late Mr. Thomas Cardew, an old gentleman of a very charitable and kindly disposition, found me, and gave me the name of Worthing, because he happened to have a first-class ticket for Worthing in his pocket at the time. Worthing is a place in Sussex. It is a seaside resort.

LADY BRACKNELL: Where did the charitable gentleman who had a first-class ticket for this seaside resort find you?

JACK: In a hand-bag.[62]

LADY BRACKNELL: [63] A hand-bag!

JACK: Yes, [64] Lady Bracknell. I was in a hand-bag—a somewhat large, black leather hand-bag, with handles to it—an ordinary hand-bag in fact.

LADY BRACKNELL: In what locality did this Mr. James, or Thomas, Cardew come across this ordinary hand-bag?

JACK: [65] In the cloak-room at Victoria Station. It was given to him in mistake for his own.

LADY BRACKNELL: The cloak-room at Victoria Station?[66]

JACK: Yes. [67] The Brighton line.

LADY BRACKNELL: The line is immaterial. [68] Mr. Worthing, I confess I feel somewhat bewildered by what you have just told me. To be born, or at any rate bred, in a hand-bag, whether it had handles or not, seems to me to display a contempt for the ordinary decencies of family life that reminds one of the worst excesses of the French Revolution. And I presume you know what that unfortunate movement led to? As for the particular locality in which the hand-bag was found, a cloak-room at a railway station might serve to conceal a social indiscretion—has probably, indeed, been used for that purpose before now—but it could hardly be regarded as an assured basis for a recognized position in good society.

JACK: [69] May I ask you then what you would advise me to do? I need hardly say I would do anything in the world to ensure Gwendolen's happiness.

[70] Opens her notebook to review the information.

[71] Closes her notebook forcefully.

[72] Exits up right as she passes in front of him. He tries to stop her at the door and then retreats to the table, where he picks up several sandwiches and slumps in the chair, munching.

LADY BRACKNELL: [70] I would strongly advise you, Mr. Worthing, to try and acquire some relations as soon as possible, and to make a definite effort to produce at any rate one parent, of either sex, before the season is quite over.

JACK: Well, I don't see how I could possible manage to do that. I can produce the hand-bag at any moment. It is in my dressing room at home. I really think that should satisfy you, Lady Bracknell.

LADY BRACKNELL: Me, [71] sir! What has it to do with me? You can hardly imagine that I and Lord Bracknell would dream of allowing our only daughter—a girl brought up with the utmost care—to marry into a cloak-room, and form an alliance with a hand-bag! Good morning, [72] Mr. Worthing!

Gwendolen Fairfax, the young lady from the city, has decided to pay a visit to Cecily Cardew, a most attractive and innocent young girl who has always resided in the seclusion of the country. Each is now engaged to be married to a gentleman who calls himself Ernest Worthing, the name assumed by both Jack and his friend Algernon because it is so appealing to the ladies' romantic imagination.

It is the first meeting of the two, and each is very careful to appear refined, elegant, and worldly. Although as the scene progresses it becomes apparent that they may be engaged to the same gentleman, both Gwendolen and Cecily are conscious that they must still exhibit social grace and decorum.

The humor of the situation, compounded by a series of misunderstandings and suspicions, is highlighted by the frequent references to individual diaries to verify the truth of the respective engagements. Beginning actors should approach the scene with honesty and restraint to reveal the triviality of the skirmish.

As the scene begins, Cecily is placing some books on the table down left. She sits and turns the pages, and then rises to move to the rosebush up right. Picking a rose, she turns to the table and is gazing into the distance with dreamy eyes as Gwendolen enters from up right. Sensing that someone is staring at her, Cecily turns slowly and speaks.

ACT II

Cast:

Cecily

Gwendolen

Scene:

Garden at the Manor House. A flight of gray stone steps leads up to the house. The garden, an old-fashioned one, is full of roses. Time of year, July. Basket chairs and a table covered with books are set under a large yew tree.

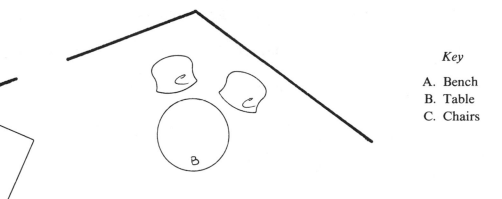

Key

A. Bench
B. Table
C. Chairs

[1] Placing the rose on the table, she steps forward.

[2] Crosses to center.

[3] Crosses to her, as they shake hands.

[4] They cross to the bench and sit, with Cecily on the right. They open parasols and study each other very closely.

[5] Rises to cross behind the bench and then to the table down left.

[6] Rises to cross center.

[7] Takes out her reading glasses as Cecily rushes to the bench to pose.

CECILY: [1] Pray let me introduce myself to you. My name is Cecily Cardew.

GWENDOLEN: Cecily Cardew? [2] What a very sweet name! Something tells me that we are going to be great friends. I like you already more than I can say. My first impressions of people are never wrong.

CECILY: [3] How nice of you to like me so much after we have known each other such a comparatively short time. Pray sit down.[4]

GWENDOLEN: I may call you Cecily, may I not?

CECILY: With pleasure!

GWENDOLEN: And you will always call me Gwendolen, won't you?

CECILY: If you wish.

GWENDOLEN: Then that is all quite settled, is it not?

CECILY: I hope so.

GWENDOLEN: Perhaps this might be a favourable opportunity for my mentioning who I am. My father is Lord Bracknell. You have heard of papa, I suppose?

CECILY: I don't think so.[5]

GWENDOLEN: Outside the family circle, [6] papa, I am glad to say, is entirely unknown. I think that is quite as it should be. The home seems to me to be the proper sphere for the man. And certainly once a man begins to neglect his domestic duties he becomes painfully effeminate, does he not? And I don't like that. It makes men so very attractive. Cecily, mamma, whose views on education are remarkably strict, has brought me up to be extremely shortsighted; it is part of her system; so do you mind my looking at you through my glasses?[7]

[8] Slowly advances to the bench during the following dialogue.

[9] Staring directly into her eyes.

[10] Crosses slowly to the table to dispose of her glasses.

[11] Crosses one step to center.

[12] Crosses another step to center.

[13] Crosses another step to center.

[14] Rises.

[15] Crosses to bench, as both ladies sit.

[16] Cecily rises at the mention of his name.

[17] Rises for emphasis.

[18] Sits.

[19] Sits.

[20] Rises.

[21] Rises.

[22] Sits.

[23] Sits.

CECILY: Oh! not at all, Gwendolen. I am very fond of being looked at.

GWENDOLEN: You are here on a short visit, [8] I suppose?

CECILY: Oh, no! I live here.

GWENDOLEN: Really? Your mother, no doubt, or some female relative of advanced years, resides here also?

CECILY: Oh, no! I have no mother, nor, in fact, any relations.

GWENDOLEN: Indeed?

CECILY: My dear guardian, with the assistance of Miss Prism, has the arduous task of looking after me.

GWENDOLEN: Your guardian?[9]

CECILY: Yes, I am Mr. Worthing's ward.

GWENDOLEN: Oh! [10] It is strange he never mentioned to me that he had a ward. How secretive of him! He grows more interesting hourly. I am not sure, however, that the news inspires me with feelings of unmixed delight. I am very fond of you, Cecily; I have liked you ever since I met you! But I am bound to state that now that I know that you are Mr. Worthing's ward, I cannot help expressing a wish that you were—[11] well, just a little older than you seem to be—[12] and not quite so very alluring in appearance. In fact, [13] if I may speak candidly—

CECILY: Pray do! [14] I think that whenever one has anything unpleasant to say, one should always be quite candid.

GWENDOLEN: Well, [15] to speak with perfect candour, Cecily, I wish that you were fully forty-two, and more than usually plain for your age. [16] Ernest has a strong upright nature. He is the very soul of truth and honor. Disloyalty would be as impossible to him as deception. But even men of the noblest possible moral character are extremely susceptible to the influence of the physical charms of others. Modern, no less than Ancient History, supplies us with many most painful examples of what I refer to. If it were not so, indeed, History would be quite unreadable.[17]

CECILY: I beg your pardon, [18] Gwendolen, did you say Ernest?

GWENDOLEN: Yes.[19]

CECILY: Oh, [20] but it is not Mr. Ernest Worthing who is my guardian. It is his brother—his elder brother.

GWENDOLEN: [21] Ernest never mentioned to me that he had a brother.

CECILY: [22] I am sorry to say that they have not been on good terms for a long time.

GWENDOLEN: Ah! [23] that accounts for it. And now that I think of it I have never heard any man mention his brother. The

24 Folds parasol.

25 Folds parasol.

26 Drops parasol.

27 Pats her hand.

28 Rises and moves down right, and then turns to face her.

29 Crosses to her.

30 Produces diary from handbag and points out the entry.

31 Crosses to the table to produce her diary and points out the entry.

32 Crosses to her.

33 Crosses up center with a small dinner bell, and rings.

34 Crosses to her and takes the dinner bell, and rings louder.

35 Crosses to the table and sits, down left.

36 Crosses to the table and sits, down right.

subject seems distasteful to most men. Cecily, 24 you have lifted a load from my mind. I was growing almost anxious. It would have been terrible if any cloud had come across a friendship like ours, would it not? Of course you are quite, quite sure that it is not Mr. Ernest Worthing who is your guardian?

CECILY: Quite sure. In fact, 25 I am going to be his.

GWENDOLEN: 26 I beg your pardon?

CECILY: Dearest Gwendolen, 27 there is no reason why I should make a secret of it to you. Our little country newspaper is sure to chronicle the fact next week. Mr. Ernest Worthing and I are engaged to be married.

GWENDOLEN: My darling Cecily, 28 I think there must be some slight error. Mr. Ernest Worthing is engaged to me. The announcement will appear in the *Morning Post* on Saturday at the latest.

CECILY: 29 I am afraid you must be under some misconception. Ernest proposed to me exactly ten minutes ago.

GWENDOLEN: It is very curious, 30 for he asked me to be his wife yesterday afternoon at 5:30. If you wish to verify the incident, pray do so. I never travel without my diary. One should always have something sensational to read on the train. I am so sorry, dear Cecily, if it is any disappointment to you, but I am afraid I have the prior claim.

CECILY: 31 It would distress me more than I can tell you, dear Gwendolen, if it caused you any mental or physical anguish, but I feel bound to point out that since Ernest proposed to you he clearly has changed his mind.

GWENDOLEN: 32 If the poor fellow has been entrapped into any foolish promise I shall consider it my duty to rescue him at once, and with a firm hand.

CECILY: 33 Whatever unfortunate entanglement my dear boy may have got into, I will never reproach him with it after we are married.

GWENDOLEN: Do you allude to me, 34 Miss Cardew, as an entanglement? You are presumptuous. On an occasion of this kind it becomes more than a moral duty to speak one's mind. It becomes a pleasure.

CECILY: Do you suggest, 35 Miss Fairfax, that I entrapped Ernest into an engagement? How dare you. This is no time for wearing the shallow mask of manners. When I see a spade I call it a spade.

GWENDOLEN: 36 I am glad to say that I have never seen a spade.

[37] Enters from up right with a tea tray and small cakes. Cecily and Gwendolen resume a polite attitude as Merriman prepares to serve. He steps aside and waits as the ladies engage in a game of verbal tennis.

[38] Merriman steps to table to serve the tea and cakes.

[39] Cecily fills the cup with sugar, and Merriman places it in front of a surprised Gwendolen.

[40] Cecily cuts a large piece of cake, and Merriman places it in front of a surprised Gwendolen.

[41] Rises.

[42] Moves center.

[43] Turns to face her.

[44] Rises and then crosses to her.

[45] Opens her parasol.

It is obvious that our social spheres have been widely different.

MERRIMAN: [37] Shall I lay tea here as usual, Miss?

CECILY: Yes, as usual.

GWENDOLEN: Are there many interesting walks in the vicinity, Miss Cardew?

CECILY: Oh! yes! a great many. From the top of one of the hills quite close one can see five counties.

GWENDOLEN: Five counties! I don't think I should like that; I hate crowds.

CECILY: I suppose that is why you live in town?

GWENDOLEN: Quite a well-kept garden this is, Miss Cardew.

CECILY: So glad you like it, Miss Fairfax.

GWENDOLEN: I had no idea there were any flowers in the country.

CECILY: Oh, flowers are as common here, Miss Fairfax, as people are in London.

GWENDOLEN: Personally, I cannot understand how anybody manages to exist in the country, if anybody who is anybody does. The country always bores me to death.

CECILY: Ah! This is what the newspapers call agricultural depression, is it not? I believe the aristocracy are suffering very much from it just at present. It is almost an epidemic amongst them, I have been told. May I offer you some tea, Miss Fairfax?[38]

GWENDOLEN: Thank you. (Aside.) Detestable girl! But I require tea!

CECILY: Sugar?

GWENDOLEN: No, [39] thank you. Sugar is not fashionable any more.

CECILY: Cake or bread and butter?

GWENDOLEN: Bread and butter, [40] please. Cake is rarely seen at the best houses nowadays.

CECILY: Hand that to Miss Fairfax.

GWENDOLEN: [41] You have filled my tea with lumps of sugar, and though I asked most distinctly for bread and butter, you have given me cake. [42] I am known for the gentleness of my disposition, and the extraordinary sweetness of my nature, [43] but I warn you, Miss Cardew, you may go too far.

CECILY: To save my poor, [44] innocent, trusting boy from the machinations of any other girl there are no lengths to which I would not go.

GWENDOLEN: [45] From the moment I saw you I distrusted you. I felt that you were false and deceitful. I am never deceived

46 Crosses up right and politely gestures for Gwendolen to exit.

Gwendolen exits up right as Cecily retires to the table, opens her diary, and reads while sipping tea.

Merriman exits with tray up right.

in such matters. My first impressions of people are invariably right.

CECILY: It seems to me, 46 Miss Fairfax, that I am trespassing on your valuable time. No doubt you have many other calls of a similar character to make in the neighbourhood.

Act II

ON PLAYING MODERN SCENES

The actor's basic approach to playing modern scenes depends upon his ability to create the illusion of reality and to convince the audience that what is seen and heard is honest and natural and that it is also spontaneous and familiar.

In the selected scenes, the beginning actor should assume that an invisible "fourth wall" exists between him and his audience and should direct dialogue and reactions to the other actors within the playing area. There is no attempt in the modern acting style to engage actively with the audience other than to hold their attention and gain their approval.

Approach the playing of modern scenes by speaking and moving in a relaxed, spontaneous, and distinctly personal manner. Remember that modern plays are concerned with realistic episodes in the lives of ordinary people and that the style of performance needed to convey the thoughts and emotions of these rather common characters must be direct, subdued, and conversational.

There is little opportunity in modern scenes to imitate the style of the previous period scenes, and the beginning actor should distinguish between the period emphasis upon artificial, stilted, or formal delivery and the modern impulse to be reasonable, restrained, and rational in performance. There is also little opportunity in modern scenes to imitate the exaggerated posing, elegant movement, or pretentious speech that characterized the period attempt to suggest sophistication and "high manners."

Because modern plays are more concerned than period ones with depicting actual events or carefully drawn characters based on realistic observation, the actor is faced with the difficult, but highly creative, task known as "giving character" to his performance.

The primary concern in the art of giving character is to observe human nature and the environment and then to select those personalities, experiences, or circumstances that may be incorporated into the world of the play. This process of allowing the character of the play to be shaped by the actor's lived experiences or observed actions brings vitality and credibility to the performance and provides the actor with a role model by which to relate the events of the scene to his own understanding.

Among the more important elements to observe in seeking to give character to a role are persons of varying ages, physical dimensions, economic status, emotional or intellectual makeup, and behavioral pattern. By jotting down the observed traits in his performance "memory book," the actor can draw upon his observations and his experiences to suggest realistic walks, postures, voices, attitudes, relationships, or actions by which to convey to the audience that the character portrait is accurate and authentic.

56

This is not to imply, however, that the actor must rely solely upon observation for his performance guidelines. There are also opportunities to select one's personal traits such as physique, comic flair, vocal quality, or style of movement to give added dimension to the performance. The important point is that the actor observe what is *necessary* to suggest a realistic approach to his character, and that any personal additions be included only if they are complementary and truthful in helping to *complete* the portrait.

Additional hints for giving character to the performance may be found in an examination of the play itself, especially if the playwright has included detailed stage directions. An examination of the play will also provide the actor with important clues to relationships with other characters and to help define the character's motivation.

All of the scenes in the modern section encourage the beginning actor to use his powers of observation in creating characters that have a basis in reality. The scenes all involve a relationship of some sort and need carefully chosen personality traits to express the mood that is being suggested.

Desire Under the Elms, for example, demands a sensitive treatment of the love interest between a young man and his stepmother, who are drawn toward each other out of a sense of loneliness and despair. *A View from the Bridge* demands a tone of youthful innocence and initial frustration that often arises in relationships between persons of differing social or economic backgrounds.

The same adolescent innocence should provide a useful key for interpretation of *6 RMS RIV VU,* even though the characters in this scene are more mature. The basic approach to playing *Becket* is to observe the attitude of friends who may quarrel over an unimportant matter but still remain trusted companions. *Requiem for Romance,* on the other hand, should combine the elements of frustration and quarrelsomeness to best suggest the deteriorating family relationship of the characters.

Regardless what observed traits or personality characteristics are incorporated into the playing of the scenes, however, the actor should be reminded that modern scenes avoid overly precise use of the voice, exaggerated movement, and theatrical posing. Approach each scene with sensitivity and objectivity, employing a conversational tone of delivery, a relaxed and natural sense of movement, and an animation that suggests energy and involvement.

Always direct dialogue and subtle reactions to the other performers in the scene to highlight the intimate nature of modern scenes. It might also be useful to make a chart of your character's changing moods, attitudes, or responses to other characters, and to rehearse the most economical and believable manner in which to suggest these changes to the audience with a minimum of vocal and physical effort.

FROM

Desire Under the Elms (1924)
by EUGENE O'NEILL

The compelling and destructive power of lust and passion is the principal characteristic of this modern tragedy, symbolized by two enormous elms that brood oppressively over the New England dirt farm of Ephraim Cabot and his sons.

A stern, tyrannical old man, the elder Cabot is as hard and unbending as the stony, barren ground that surrounds his rundown house. He has already buried two wives and is now married to a third, a much younger and attractive woman named Abbie Putnam. All three sons despise their father, and two of them, Peter and Simeon, leave the farm as the play begins.

Only Eben, the youngest and most sensitive, remains. Blaming his mother's early death on his cruel father, Eben considers himself the rightful heir to the Cabot farm and is at first resentful of Abbie. As the action unfolds, however, Eben and Abbie are attracted to each other and soon discover that their passion is more intense than their struggle for possession of the farm.

Late one evening the sensuous Abbie entices Eben to join her in the family parlor, which has not been opened since Eben's mother died. She hopes to seduce him, as part of a scheme to bear a child by Eben and to deceive the elder Cabot into believing it is his, thus securing her inheritance to the property.

In playing the scene, the actor should try to capture the frustration and loneliness that has led these two tormented souls to seek each other out in the quiet of the night. Abbie's all-consuming passion leads her to taunt and tease Eben into submission, and she is coy in her attempts to seduce him. Eben is at first cautious and hesitant, more concerned with the "presence" of his mother than with the temptation presented by Abbie. Over the scene, however, hangs an air of impending doom and death.

The performers should approach the scene with calm restraint, especially in handling the New England accent. The embraces are not as forceful as the script suggests, and to exaggerate them would be to lessen the desired mood of pity and despair. The tempo of the scene is subdued and halting, and Eben should appear more nervous and suspicious than Abbie as he frequently interrupts his dialogue to glance about, hoping to catch a glimpse of his late mother's spirit.

In staging the scene, a darkened room with candles would suggest the needed mood. The performers may wish to wear ragged clothes and go barefoot in keeping with the rural, almost primitive, setting noted in the stage directions.

Cast:

Abbie
Eben

Scene:

The interior of a parlor, which resembles a tomb. It is late evening.

Desire Under the Elms

ACT II, SCENE III

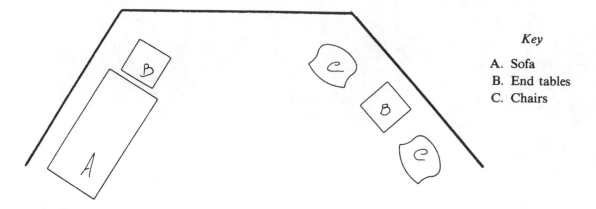

Key

A. Sofa
B. End tables
C. Chairs

The scene opens with Abbie sitting quietly on the edge of the sofa, combing her hair and awaiting the arrival of Eben. Her appearance is youthful and expectant, but there is a frightened expression on her face. Eben enters and stands staring at her, his arms hanging loosely at his sides. He carries a hat.

After a prolonged and awkward moment of silence, Abbie speaks. Throughout the scene there is a nervous, formal politeness between the two, and both remain somewhat rigid, altering positions to avoid the knowing glances that are cast between them. In the dim light, they appear more like ghosts than man and woman, and their voices often trail off in whispers.

At the opening, Abbie is seated on the sofa, right. Eben enters and stands extreme down left.

[1] Crosses and sits on the sofa, left, so their eyes do not meet.

[2] Places her hand on the seat in the center of the sofa.

[3] Inches her hand close to Eben's.

[4] Faces him and strains her body forward.

[5] Inches her hand closer.

ABBIE: (after a pause—with a nervous, formal politeness) Won't ye set?

EBEN: (dully) [1] Ay-eh.
(Mechanically he places his hat carefully on the floor near the door and sits stiffly beside her on the edge of the sofa. A pause. They both remain rigid, looking straight ahead with eyes full of fear.)

ABBIE: [2] When I fust come in—in the dark—they seemed t' somethin' here.

EBEN: (simply) Maw.

ABBIE: [3] I kin still feel—somethin' . . .

EBEN: It's Maw.

ABBIE: [4] At fust I was feered o' it. I wanted t' yell an' run. Now— since yew come—seems like it's growin' soft and kind t' me. (Addressing the air—queerly) Thank yew.

EBEN: Maw allus loved me.

ABBIE: Mebbe it knows I love yew, [5] too. Mebbe that makes it kind t' me.

[6] Unconsciously places his hand on the sofa.

[7] Abbie places her hand on his.

[8] Slowly glances at her hand and then turns away.

[9] Slowly rises.

[10] Slides over on the sofa and tries to grasp Eben's hand.

[11] Pulls away and moves down center.

[12] Draws Eben back to the sofa, and they sit as before.

[13] Putting one arm over his shoulder. He does not seem to notice.

[14] Eben places his hand on Abbie's shoulder, very slowly.

[15] Abbie places her hand on Eben's shoulder, very slowly.

[16] Softly in his ear.

[17] Whispers softly, her lips almost touching his ear.

[18] Places both of her arms round him, with wild passion.

[19] Eben lies on the sofa with his head on Abbie's lap, facing downstage.

[20] On his back, looking directly into Abbie's face.

EBEN: (dully) [6] I dunno. I should think she'd hate ye.

ABBIE: (with certainty) No. [7] I kin feel it don't—not no more.

EBEN: [8] Hate ye fur stealin' her place—here in her hum—settin' in her parlor whar she was laid—(He suddenly stops, staring stupidly before him.)

ABBIE: What is it, Eben?

EBEN: (in a whisper) [9] Seems like Maw didn't want me t' remind ye.

ABBIE: (excitedly) I knowed, [10] Eben! It's kind t' me! It don't b'ar me no grudges fur what I never knowed an' couldn't help!

EBEN: Maw b'ars him a grudge.

ABBIE: Waal, so does all o' us.

EBEN: Ay-eh. [11] (With passion) I does, by God!

ABBIE: [12] Thar. Don't git riled thinkin' o' him. Think o' yer Maw who's kind t' us. Tell me about yer Maw, Eben.

EBEN: They hain't nothin' much. She was kind. She was good.

ABBIE: [13] I'll be kind an' good t' ye!

EBEN: [14] Sometimes she used t' sing fur me.

ABBIE: I'll sing fur ye!

EBEN: This was her hum. This was her farm.

ABBIE: This is my hum! [15] This is my farm!

EBEN: He married her t' steal 'em. She was soft an' easy. He couldn't 'preciate her.

ABBIE: [16] He can't 'preciate me!

EBEN: He murdered her with his hardness.

ABBIE: [17] He's murderin' me!

EBEN: She died. (A pause) Sometimes she used to sing fur me. (He bursts into a fit of sobbing.)

ABBIE: [18] I'll sing fur ye! I'll die fur ye!

(In spite of her overwhelming desire for him, there is a sincere maternal love in her manner and voice a horribly frank mixture of lust and motherly love.)

Don't cry, [19] Eben! I'll take yer Maw's place! I'll be everythin' she was t' ye! Let me kiss ye, Eben!

(She pulls his head around. He makes a bewildered pretense of resistance. She is tender.)

[20] Don't be afeered! I'll kiss ye pure, Eben—same's if I was a Maw t' ye—an' ye kin kiss me back 's if yew was my son—my boy—sayin' goodnight t' me! Kiss me, Eben!

(They kiss in restrained fashion. Then suddenly wild passion overcomes her. She kisses him lustfully again and again and he flings his arms about her and returns her kisses.

²¹ Rises and crosses down center.

²² Leans forward on the sofa, her arms outstretched toward Eben.

²³ Kneels and opens his arms to the sky in prayer.

²⁴ Slides off the sofa onto the floor and crawls slowly toward him.

²⁵ Lowers his arms.

²⁶ Kneels behind him and then presses him to her bosom.

²⁷ Stands abruptly.

²⁸ Takes her hand and gently lowers her to her knees, in a position similar to that of a couple at the altar.

²⁹ They sink slowly to the floor as the lights fade.

Suddenly, as in the bedroom, he frees himself from her violently and springs to his feet. ²¹ He is trembling all over, in a strange state of terror. ABBIE strains her arms toward him with fierce pleading.)

²² Don't leave me, Eben! Can't ye see it hain't enuf—lovin' ye like a Maw—can't ye see it's got t' be that an' more—much more—a hundred times more—fur me t' be happy—fur yew t' be happy?

EBEN: (to the presence he feels in the room) Maw! ²³ Maw! What d' ye want? What air ye tellin' me?

ABBIE: ²⁴ She's tellin' ye t' love me. She knows I love ye an' I'll be good t' ye. Can't ye feel it? Don't ye know? She's tellin' ye t' love me, Eben!

EBEN: Ay-eh. ²⁵ I feel—mebbe she—but—I can't figger out—why—when ye've stole her place—here in her hum—in the parlor whar she was—

ABBIE: (fiercely) ²⁶ She knows I love ye!

EBEN: (his face suddenly lighting up with a fierce, triumphant grin) I see it! I see why. It's her vengeance on him—so's she kin rest quiet in her grave!

ABBIE: (wildly) ²⁷ Vengeance o' God on the hull o' us! What d' we give a durn? I love ye, Eben! God knows I love ye!

(She stretches out her arms for him.)

EBEN: (throws himself on his knees beside the sofa and grabs her in his arms—releasing all his pent-up passion)

An' I love yew, Abbie!—now I kin say it! ²⁸ I been dyin' fur want o' ye—every hour since ye come! ²⁹ I love ye!

(Their lips meet in a fierce, bruising kiss.)

FROM

A View from the Bridge (1955)
by ARTHUR MILLER

Against the social backdrop of poverty, illegal aliens, and decaying Old World morality, this tragic drama weaves the sympathetic story of a "common man" hero, Eddie Carbonne, whose fierce desire for something better in a world of tenements and slums eventually leads to violence and death.

Eddie, a hard-working longshoreman, is struggling to support his wife, Beatrice, and his orphaned niece, Catherine. When two of his wife's cousins, even poorer than he, are smuggled into the country from Sicily, Eddie gives them shelter in his house.

The niece and the strikingly handsome younger cousin, Rodolpho, fall in love and want to marry, but Eddie opposes the marriage and refuses to give permission for the niece to leave. Driven nearly mad by his own repressed desire for Catherine, Eddie then accuses Rodolpho of wanting to marry only so that he may obtain American citizenship.

When this accusation fails to persuade Catherine to abandon her lover, Eddie reports the illegal immigrants to the authorities. Before being deported, however, the elder cousin, Marco, kills Eddie and avenges the betrayal, leaving the audience to ponder what is to become of Beatrice, Catherine, and Rodolpho.

In playing the scene, the actors should keep in mind the sense of outrage that both Catherine and Rodolpho feel in their relationship with the bitter and sarcastic Eddie. Catherine, even though she truly loves Rodolpho, feels guilty about leaving Eddie after all that he has done for her; she wishes that Rodolpho could be more tolerant and understanding of Eddie's violent outbursts.

Rodolpho, puzzled about the true intent of Eddie's concern for Catherine, is furious about the innuendoes that have been whispered about the docks concerning his masculinity. He is also upset that Catherine is not strong enough to break the ties that bind her to the Carbonne household.

There is an uneasiness in the scene as Catherine and Rodolpho find themselves alone for the first time. She is seeking to express herself cautiously, not knowing what Rodolpho's response might be; and he is at first hurt and then angry at what he believes she is suggesting. The verbal exchanges, however, give way to a happy and peaceful conclusion as each realizes that their love is stronger than any obstacle they may face.

Cast:

Catherine
Rodolpho

Scene:

The interior of the Carbonne apartment, around supper time.

ACT II

As the scene opens, Catherine is arranging a paper dress pattern on the kitchen table and carelessly beginning the preparations for the evening meal. Rodolpho, who has not found work this day, is watching her intently. Occasionally, they steal glances back and forth and then smile uncomfortably.

Both are timid and shy, especially since they are alone in the apartment for the first time. Catherine is deliberate and carefully searches for the right words; Rodolpho is apparently thinking of romantic matters, especially when he begins to hum the tune of "Paper Doll."

The tone of the scene is serious, and the actors are reminded that this is an intimate, secretive conversation in which two young people confess for the first time that they are in love.

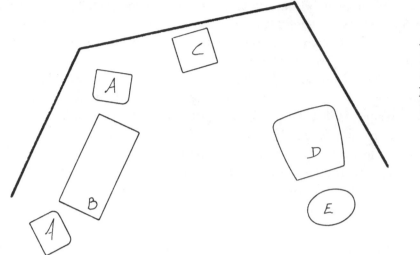

Key

A. Kitchen chairs
B. Kitchen table
C. End table
D. Rocker
E. Footstool

At the opening, Catherine is standing up right of the table, and Rodolpho is seated in a chair, down left.

[1] Sits upright and leans his chin on his arm. He is unable to see Catherine's face.

[2] Moves to the table and begins to peel onions.

[3] Rises.

[4] Spreads kitchen tools on the table.

[5] Faces her.

[6] Looks down at the table as she peels onions.

[7] Crosses half way to the table.

[8] Cutting the onions into small wedges.

[9] Crosses to her and takes her knife.

[10] Backs away several steps, holding the knife.

[11] Returns the knife to Catherine and crosses down left.

[12] Placing the onion wedges in a plastic container.

CATHERINE: You hungry?

RODOLPHO: [1] Not for anything to eat. (Pause.) I have nearly three hundred dollars, Catherine.

CATHERINE: [2] I heard you.

RODOLPHO: You don't like to talk about it any more?

CATHERINE: Sure, I don't mind talkin' about it.

RODOLPHO: What worries you, [3] Catherine?

CATHERINE: [4] I been wantin' to ask you about something. Could I?

RODOLPHO: All the answers are in my eyes, [5] Catherine. But you don't look in my eyes lately. You're full of secrets.

(She looks at him. She seems withdrawn.)

What is the question?

CATHERINE: [6] Suppose I wanted to live in Italy?

RODOLPHO: (smiling at the incongruity) [7] You going to marry somebody rich?

CATHERINE: No, [8] I mean live there—you and me.

RODOLPHO: (his smile vanishing.) [9] When?

CATHERINE: Well . . . when we get married.

RODOLPHO: (astonished.) [10] You want to be an Italian?

CATHERINE: No, but I could live there without being Italian. Americans live there.

RODOLPHO: Forever?

CATHERINE: Yeah.

RODOLPHO: (crosses to rocker.) You're fooling.[11]

CATHERINE: No, [12] I mean it.

[13] Turns to face her.

[14] Crosses to the left of table.

[15] Begins to chop vegetables.

[16] Takes a step toward her.

[17] She chops a bit faster.

[18] He angrily crosses down right.

[19] She chops a bit faster.

[20] He crosses to the table and leans on it.

[21] Her chopping has now built to a climax, as he tries desperately to explain and she tries desperately to understand.

[22] Catherine stops chopping.

[23] Rodolpho crosses above the table and stands beside her.

[24] She slowly turns to face him. They are now nose to nose.

[25] He crosses angrily to rocker, down left.

[26] She follows him half way, stopping center.

[27] Turns to face her.

[28] Takes a step toward him.

[29] Whirls and sits on stool, facing downstage.

[30] She crosses to him, placing her hands on his shoulders.

RODOLPHO: Where do you get such an idea?

CATHERINE: Well, you're always saying it's so beautiful there, with the mountains and the oceans and all the—

RODOLPHO: [13] You're fooling me.

CATHERINE: I mean it.

RODOLPHO: (goes to her slowly.) Catherine, [14] if I ever brought you home with no money, no business, nothing, they would call the priest and the doctor and they would say Rodolpho is crazy.

CATHERINE: I know, [15] but I think we would be happier there.

RODOLPHO: Happier! [16] What would you eat? You can't cook the view!

CATHERINE: [17] Maybe you could be a singer, like in Rome or—

RODOLPHO: Rome! [18] Rome is full of singers.

CATHERINE: Well, [19] I could work then.

RODOLPHO: Where?[20]

CATHERINE: God, [21] there must be jobs somewhere!

RODOLPHO: There's nothing. Nothing, nothing, nothing. Now tell me what you're talking about. How can I bring you from a rich country to suffer in a poor country? What are you talking about?

(She searches for words.)

I would be a criminal stealing your face. In two years you would have an old, hungry face. When my brother's babies cry they give them water, water that boiled a bone. Don't you believe that?

CATHERINE: (quietly.) [22] I'm afraid of Eddie here.

(Slight pause.)

RODOLPHO: (steps closer to her.) [23] We wouldn't live here. Once I am a citizen I could work anywhere and I would find better jobs and we would have a house, Catherine. If I were not afraid to be arrested I would start to be something wonderful here!

CATHERINE: (steeling herself.) [24] Tell me something. I mean just tell me, Rodolpho—would you still want to do it if it turned out we had to go live in Italy? I mean just if it turned out that way?

RODOLPHO: [25] This is your question or his question?

CATHERINE: I would like to know, [26] Rodolpho. I mean it.

RODOLPHO: [27] To go there with nothing.

CATHERINE: Yeah.[28]

RODOLPHO: No. [29] (She looks at him wide-eyed.) No.

CATHERINE: You wouldn't?[30]

³¹ Springs up and grabs her shoulders.

³² Crosses quickly down right.

³³ She slowly turns to face him.

³⁴ Storms to center stage, then right, and finally down right.

³⁵ Sits in chair, stage right, and faces downstage.

³⁶ Crosses to him.

³⁷ Kneels and looks up at him.

³⁸ Touches her face.

³⁹ Takes his hand and gently kisses it.

⁴⁰ Rises and crosses to behind the rocker.

⁴¹ Starts to collapse and grabs the chair to keep from falling.

⁴² Rushes to her.

⁴³ Falls in his arms.

⁴⁴ Caresses her head as he holds her.

⁴⁵ She pushes him away and starts to cross down left.

⁴⁶ He grabs her arm and pulls her to him.

⁴⁷ She remains firm and stamps her foot.

RODOLPHO: No; ³¹ I will not marry you to live in Italy. I want you to be my wife, and I want to be a citizen. Tell him that, or I will. Yes.

(He moves about angrily.)

³² And tell him also, and tell yourself, please, that I am not a beggar, and you are not a horse, a gift, a favor for a poor immigrant.

CATHERINE: Well, ³³ don't get mad!

RODOLPHO: I am furious! ³⁴ (Goes to her.) Do you think I am so desperate? My brother is desperate, not me. You think I would carry on my back the rest of my life a woman I didn't love just to be an American? It's so wonderful? You think we have no tall buildings in Italy? Electric lights? No wide streets? No flags? No automobiles? ³⁵ Only work we don't have. I want to be an American so I can work, that is the only wonder here—work! How can you insult me, Catherine?

CATHERINE: I didn't mean that—³⁶

RODOLPHO: My heart dies to look at you. Why are you so afraid of him?

CATHERINE: (near tears) ³⁷ I don't know!

RODOLPHO: Do you trust me, ³⁸ Catherine?

CATHERINE: ³⁹ It's only that I—He was good to me, Rodolpho. You don't know him; he was always the sweetest guy to me. Good. He razzes me all the time but he don't mean it. I know. I would—just feel ashamed if I made him sad. ⁴⁰ 'Cause I always dreamt that when I got married he would be happy at the wedding, and laughin'—and now he's mad all the time and nasty—

(She is weeping.)

Tell him you'd live in Italy—just tell him and maybe he would start to trust you a little, see? Because I want him to be happy; I mean—⁴¹ I like him, Rodolpho—and I can't stand it!

RODOLPHO: Oh, ⁴² Catherine—oh, little girl.

CATHERINE: I love you, ⁴³ Rodolpho, I love you.

RODOLPHO: ⁴⁴ Then why are you afraid? That he'll spank you?

CATHERINE: Don't, ⁴⁵ don't laugh at me! I've been here all my life. Every day I saw him when he left in the morning and when he came home at night. You think it's so easy to turn around and say to a man he's nothing to you no more?

RODOLPHO: I know, ⁴⁶ but—

CATHERINE: You don't know; ⁴⁷ nobody knows! I'm not a baby, I know a lot more than people think I know. Beatrice says to be a woman, but—

[48] He gently kisses her hand.

[49] Slowly moving toward him, teasing as she walks.

[50] He cups her face in his hands.

[51] She throws her arms around him.

[52] He kisses her tenderly and then scoops her up in his arms and carries her off up left.

RODOLPHO: [48] Yes.

CATHERINE: Then why don't she be a woman? [49] If I was a wife I would make a man happy instead of goin' at him all the time. I can tell when he's hungry or wants a beer before he even says anything. I know when his feet hurt him, I mean I know him and now I'm supposed to turn around and make a stranger out of him? I don't know why I have to do that, I mean.

RODOLPHO: Catherine. [50] If I take in my hands a little bird. And she grows and wishes to fly. But I will not let her out of my hands because I love her so much, is that right for me to do? I don't say you must hate him; but anyway you must go, mustn't you? Catherine?

CATHERINE: (softly.) [51] Hold me.

RODOLPHO: (clasping her to him.) Oh, my little girl.

CATHERINE: Teach me. (She is weeping.) I don't know anything. Teach me, Rodolpho, hold me.

RODOLPHO: [52] There's nobody here now. Come inside. Come. (He is leading her toward the bedrooms.) And don't cry any more.

FROM

Becket, or the Honor of God (1959)
by JEAN ANOUILH
translated by LUCIENNE HILL

Although it has for its subject the conflict between church and state, this drama reflects neither decidedly religious views nor Christian principles of charity and virtue. Instead, it is a play that explores the rivalry between two strong-willed men who find themselves in conflict over the more human questions of personal integrity and loyalty.

Beginning as a flashback of the early love-hate relationship between King Henry II of England and his trusted servant and comrade Thomas à Becket, the drama details the alternating pleasure and pain they shared during their adolescence and emerging manhood.

The basic conflict revolves around Becket who, at the King's urging, is appointed Archbishop of Canterbury. In the new position as spiritual curate, Becket's loyalties suddenly change without apparent reason, and he begins to challenge his ruler's right to reign over both church and state. The resulting struggle for power ends eventually in Becket's martyrdom and King Henry's sorrow.

In playing the scene, the actors should capture the jesting innocence and youthful rebellion that often mark young men approaching adulthood. They should also suggest the competitive jealousy and suspicion that young men often feel when they regard close friends as possible rivals for attention and recognition.

King Henry should be played as a rather rough, simple-hearted fellow who just happens to find himself in the unique position of ruling England. There should be an almost doglike affection and earnest attempt to please in the devotion of the more athletic and handsome Becket.

The mood of the scene is one of urgency and expectation, as Henry awaits the tardy arrival of his friend, while Becket is somewhat cautious and suspicious of the King's unexpected summons. It might even be said that the confrontation between the two resembles a chess game, with first the King and then Becket scheming strategic moves and countermoves to force the other into submission.

As the scene concludes, it should be obvious to the audience that King Henry, for the first time, is clearly in a dominant position in his relationship with Becket, and that Becket is no longer a trusted friend.

Cast

King
Becket

Scene:

The King's tent, set up among trees in a secluded forest in France. It is dawn, and a stillness is upon the early morning.

ACT II

The scene opens in a mood of hushed anticipation, as Becket has just arrived in France to speak with the King concerning the movement of English soldiers. The King is at first

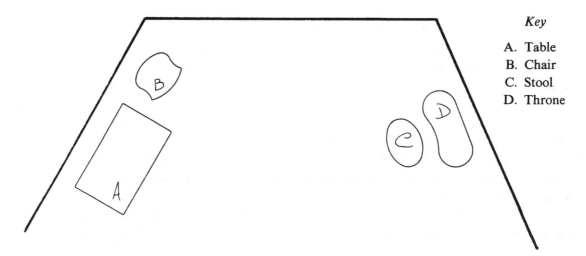

Key

A. Table
B. Chair
C. Stool
D. Throne

cautious, not knowing whether Becket is still a true and loyal friend. But it should be obvious at first glance that the two are comrades, even though they have not seen each other for some time.

The actors are reminded that the King is somewhat childish in his attitude, and that he is playing a game with Becket to test his friendship and loyalty. Becket, on the other hand, is naive and completely unaware that the King has summoned him to France to make him Archbishop.

As the scene opens, Becket is standing at the table looking at a book.

[1] Storms in from up left.

[2] Becket turns, and then bows.

[3] Stops center stage.

[4] Unconsciously crosses himself.

[5] Crosses to him and pats his shoulder rather roughly.

[6] Crosses a few steps down center.

[7] Fiercely holds Becket by the shoulders and shakes him.

[8] Crosses to the throne, and unceremoniously sits down.

[9] Crosses halfway to him, hesitantly.

[10] Crosses a few more steps toward him.

KING: Becket![1]

BECKET: [2] Everything is going according to plan, my prince. The troops are on their way. We've only to wait here quietly, until they arrive.

KING: (Cheerfully) You're right, [3] Becket, everything is going according to plan. God isn't angry with us. He has just recalled the Archbishop.

BECKET: (In a murmur) [4] That little old man ... How could that feeble body contain so much strength?

KING: Now, [5] now, now! Don't squander your sorrow, my son. I personally consider this an excellent piece of news!

BECKET: [6] He was the first Norman who took an interest in me. He was a true father to me. God rest his soul.

KING: He will! [7] After all the fellow did for Him, he's gone to heaven, don't worry. Where he'll be definitely more use to God than he was to us. So it's definitely for the best.

He pulls BECKET to him.

Becket! [8] My little Becket, I think the ball's in our court now! This is the time to score a point.

He seizes his arm, tense and quite transformed.

An extraordinary idea is just creeping into my mind, Becket. A master stroke! I can't think what's got into me this morning, but I suddenly feel extremely intelligent. It probably comes of making love with a French girl last night. I am subtle, Becket, I am profound! So profound it's making my head spin. Are you sure it isn't dangerous to think too hard? Thomas, my little Thomas! Are you listening to me?

BECKET: (Smiling at his excitement) Yes, [9] my prince.

KING: (As excited as a little boy) Are you listening carefully? Listen, Thomas! You told me once that the best ideas are the stupidest ones, but the clever thing is to think of them! Listen, Thomas! Tradition prevents me from touching the privileges of the Primacy. You follow me so far?

BECKET: Yes, [10] my prince.

KING: But what if the Primate is my man? If the Archbishop

[11] Kicks the stool upstage and then motions for Becket to sit near him.

[12] Becket crosses to stool and returns with it, to sit near the King.

[13] Extends his hand as he gestures.

[14] Pounds the arm of the throne.

[15] Leans forward suddenly and grabs Becket by the coat. Slowly the King pulls Becket forward until they both teeter precariously on the edge of their seats, with noses almost touching.

[16] Releases him abruptly.

[17] Rises.

[18] Smiles with difficulty.

[19] Begins to laugh, rather loudly.

[20] Becket strikes a few dancing poses and waltzes about in a comic gait.

[21] The laughter builds until the King suddenly ends it with a loud clap of his hands.

of Canterbury is for the King, how can his power possibly incommodate me?[11]

BECKET: That's an ingenious idea, [12] my prince, but you forget that his election is a free one.

KING: No! [13] You're forgetting the Royal Hand! Do you know what that is? When the candidate is displeasing to the Throne the King sends his Justicer to the Conclave of Bishops and it's the King who has the final say. [14] That's an old custom, too, and for once, it's in my favor! It's fully a hundred years since the Conclave of Bishops has voted contrary to the wishes of the King!

BECKET: I don't doubt it, my Lord. But we all know your Bishops. Which one of them could you rely on? Once the Primate's miter is on their heads, they grow dizzy with power.

KING: Are you asking me, [15] Becket? I'll tell you. Someone who doesn't know what dizziness means. Someone who isn't even afraid of God. Thomas, my son, I need your help again and this time it's important. I'm sorry to deprive you of French girls and the fun of battle, my son, but pleasure will come later. You are going over to England.

BECKET: I am at your service, my prince.

KING: [16] Can you guess what your mission will be?

A tremor of anguish crosses BECKET's face at what is to come.

BECKET: No, [17] my prince.

KING: You are going to deliver a personal letter from me to every Bishop in the land. And do you know what those letters will contain, my Thomas, my little brother? My royal wish to have you elected Primate of England.

BECKET has gone deathly white. He says with a forced laugh:

BECKET: You're joking, [18] of course, my Lord. Just look at the edifying man, the saintly man whom you would be trusting with these holy functions!

He has opened his fine coat to display his even finer doublet. Why, [19] my prince, you really fooled me for a second!

The KING bursts out laughing. BECKET laughs too, rather too loudly in his relief.

A fine Archbishop I'd have made! [20] Look at my new shoes! They're the latest fashion in Paris. Attractive, that little upturned toe, don't you think? [21] Quite full of unction and compunction, isn't it, Sire?

KING: (Suddenly stops laughing) Shut up about your shoes,

²² Backing away slowly.

²³ Rising, with a stern manner.

²⁴ Kneels in supplication.

²⁵ Crosses to throne, and this time sits in a regal pose.

²⁶ Raises his head to face the King.

²⁷ Turns away slowly and whispers as the lights fade.

Thomas! I'm in deadly earnest. I shall write those letters before noon. You will help me.

BECKET, deathly pale, stammers:

BECKET: But my Lord, [22] I'm not even a priest!

KING: (Tersely) [23] You're a deacon. You can take your final vows tomorrow and be ordained in a month.

BECKET: But [24] have you considered what the Pope will say?

KING: (Brutally) I'll pay the price![25]

BECKET, after an anguished pause, murmurs:

BECKET: My Lord, [26] I see now that you weren't joking. Don't do this.

KING: Why not?

BECKET: It frightens me.

KING: (His face set and hard) Becket, this is an order!

BECKET stands as if turned to stone. A pause. He murmurs:

BECKET: (Gravely) If I become Archbishop, [27] I can no longer be your friend.

FROM

6 RMS RIV VU (1973)
by BOB RANDALL

This modern "romantic" comedy is a charming misadventure in the lonely lives of two middle-class suburbanites who meet and fall in love when answering an advertisement for an apartment in New York City.

Although both are married, they immediately sense in each other the "dream" person of their fantasies, and they agree, somewhat hesitantly, to meet in the apartment later to explore the possibilities of having a secret relationship.

What emerges from their rendezvous is a bitter-sweet love story and comic interlude, of sympathetic understanding, gentle and tender exploration of feelings, and considerable sorrow. Nevertheless, the hope is expressed that brave, honest people may yet find happiness and comfort if they continue the search and never yield to frustration or temptation.

Anne, the rather plain-looking woman, is really charming and gracious in her efforts to overcome adversity and exhibits a quiet strength and fierce independence that arouses sympathy and compassion. Paul, the would-be writer, is a harmless, heroic dreamer who believes himself more misunderstood than mistreated; he takes special delight, it seems, in recounting his "almost" intrigues and adventures in life.

In playing the scene, the actors should recall that this is the first time either Anne or Paul have actually thought of having an affair, and that each is at first nervous and unsure and then comfortable and relaxed. They should also suggest that both discover, in spite of initial misgivings and doubts, a great capacity to love.

6 RMS RIV VU

Perhaps the most difficult task in this scene is to convey the elements of tenderness and genuine concern that Anne and Paul experience as they learn of each other's emotionally empty home life. The actors should refrain from appearing bitter or sarcastic when referring to the absent spouses.

The mood of the scene should be one of lightness and gentleness, with moments of awkward intrigue and misunderstanding treated with restraint. Remember that what the characters discover about themselves in this scene is an almost spiritual capacity to understand and to love another human being, and that their apparent despair is only the failure to have been capable of doing that earlier in life.

Cast:

    Anne

    Paul

Scene:

    The empty living room of a large apartment on Riverside Drive, New York City. It is late evening, and the sound of thunder can be heard.

ACT II, SCENE II

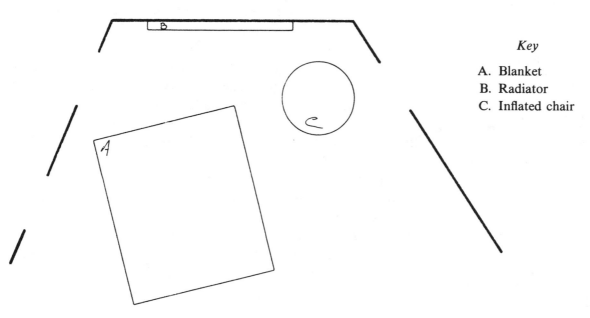

Key

A. Blanket
B. Radiator
C. Inflated chair

    The scene opens in darkness, with Anne standing in the open front door wearing a dripping raincoat. She calls softly and then takes a few hesitant steps into the room. Nervously, she feels around the wall for the light switch and then slowly removes her coat as she surveys the room. She is clutching her coat in the center of the empty room when Paul appears at the door, carrying assorted shopping bags and parcels.

    They stand staring at one another for a prolonged moment, each obviously embarrassed and unsure who should speak or move first. The initial conversation is polite and informal, the light exchanges one might expect of married men or women out on a daring adventure without their spouse. There is also the festive mood of an impromptu party as the picnic supplies are spread on the floor.

[1] Calling from offstage, down right.

[2] Knocks on the door.

ANNE: Paul? [1] Are you in there? (She checks her watch.) Eight o'clock. Ready or not, here I come. (She takes a small step into the room.) Paul?[2]

    (She feels around the wall for the light switch and turns on the overhead light. She comes into the room, goes to

³ Paces the entire length of the room.

⁴ Crosses stage left and poses casually to the audience.

⁵ Standing in the doorway.

⁶ Relaxing her pose.

⁷ Steps to center stage.

⁸ Drops his coat on the floor by the radiator, takes the bags center stage and places them on the floor.

⁹ Cautiously moving to center stage to inspect the bags.

¹⁰ Produces a blanket and gives Anne two corners of it. They shake it, position it several times, and then are satisfied with its placement centerstage.

¹¹ They kneel up center of the blanket. Anne is on the left, Paul on the right. The bags are on Anne's left.

¹² Snatches bag from her and places it dramatically on his right.

¹³ Reaches across her to grab all of the fruit bags and places them on his right.

¹⁴ He hands her each of the items with a flourish. She takes each item, inspects it carefully, and then places it on the blanket in a decorative pattern.

the bedroom hall and turns on the light switch there.) All right, I'll start without him.

(She approaches the dining room nervously, tiptoes in quickly and turns on the lights, then returns to the living room. She paces the room.)

Three, ³ six, nine, twelve, fifteen, eighteen, twenty-one, twenty-three. You haven't changed a bit. What am I doing here, meeting a man I hardly know for a picnic on the floor of an empty rent-controlled apartment? ⁴ Dear Rose Franzblau, my problem is this . . .

(ANNE starts to leave, gets to the front door where she hears PAUL coming from the elevator. She rushes back into the room and does a little "twist" step as she goes which causes her skirt to fall to its full length, revealing the long green gown she has worn for the occasion. ⁵ PAUL appears in the doorway laden down with three shopping bags and a smaller brown paper bag.)

PAUL: I'm sorry I'm late, but the Hadassah was holding a buy-in at the A&P. You came.

ANNE: ⁶ So did you. What on earth have you got there?⁷

PAUL: ⁸ (Kicks the door shut, takes off his coat and lays the bags down.) Supper.

ANNE: Is your wife's group joining us?

PAUL: No, thank God. When I last saw the ladies of liberation they were starting on their third pitcher of whiskey sours.

(He has by now taken five full paper bags out of one of the shopping bags.)

ANNE: (Looking at the bags.) I have a riddle for you. ⁹ What comes in a hundred paper bags that two people could possibly eat in one sitting?

PAUL: (Spreading a blanket on the floor.) Yeah. ¹⁰ I guess it's a little more than we need, but I didn't know what you liked.

ANNE: (Opening one of the bags.) ¹¹ Five apples? We going to bob?

PAUL: ¹² They were two pounds for forty-nine, so I got two pounds.

ANNE: (Opening another bag.) And two pounds of oranges.

PAUL: Also peaches, ¹³ bananas and grapes.

ANNE: (She has taken off her coat and puts it on the radiator.) Ten pounds of fruit. Did somebody die?

PAUL: (A beat, seeing her in the gown and appreciating it. He takes each item out of the bag as he describes it.)

¹⁴ And for dessert. Sara Lee. You like barbecued chicken? If

[15] Arranges her skirt and hair.

[16] Rises quickly, steps back, and reveals the contents of the remaining bag as though he were a magician.

[17] Crosses up left and begins to pump.

[18] Picks up an apple and weighs it.

[19] Pumping.

[20] Decides not to eat the apple and puts it back.

[21] Pumping.

[22] Picks up an orange.

[23] Pumping.

[24] Decides not to peel it and puts it back.

[25] Pumping.

[26] Picks up a single grape.

[27] Pumping.

[28] Decides not to eat it and puts it back.

[29] Pumping.

[30] Takes a banana.

[31] Pumping.

[32] Studies the banana.

not, I got a pastrami on rye—and a rare roast beef—with Russian—

> (Anne sits on the blanket and PAUL is aware he is in much more casual attire, then he continues taking food out of the shopping bag. The bottle of wine is in the separate small bag.)

Also, caviar, red. Sorry about that. Fritos, plastic wine glasses, bottle of wine, cole slaw, sweet peppers, plastic utensils, paper plates, napkins in the mod boutique pattern, shocking pink after dinner mints and a six-month supply of Wash 'n Dri. Did I forget anything?

ANNE: A souffle.[15]

PAUL: (Goes to other shopping bag.) Yes, I did. Wonder Woman comics, I'm a man of my word. (Takes out cassette player.) Music to dine by. I hope you like to eat by Chopin.

ANNE: I never heard To Eat by Chopin.

PAUL: We'll ignore that, shall we?

> (She has emptied the small bags of their fruit onto the blanket.)

And the final touch.[16]

> (From the third shopping bag he takes out two inflatable plastic chairs and a hand pump.)

Club chairs!

ANNE: I was afraid you'd try to make a pass at me. By the time you blow those things up you'll be lucky if you can shake my hand.

PAUL: Says you. [17] (Pumping.) Were you really afraid I'd make a pass?

ANNE: A little.[18]

PAUL: [19] So was I.

ANNE: Is that everything?[20]

PAUL: [21] Practically.

ANNE: What else?[22]

PAUL: [23] I'm not so sure I want to tell you.

ANNE: Why?[24]

PAUL: [25] I want to see how the evening goes first.

ANNE: Come on, [26] Paul, tell me.

PAUL: [27] Guess.

ANNE: A Monopoly set.[28]

PAUL: Oh, [29] damn it, do you like Monopoly, too?

ANNE: No![30]

PAUL: [31] Oh. Well, I'm glad I didn't bring one.

ANNE: A TV set?[32]

³³ Pumping.

³⁴ Tosses the banana aside, just as Paul collapses from pumping.

³⁵ Pauses for a breather.

³⁶ Picks up a peach.

³⁷ Crosses to her with the yearbook.

³⁸ Tosses peach aside and takes the yearbook.

³⁹ Almost drops the book in surprise.

⁴⁰ Crosses to up left position and resumes pumping.

⁴¹ Closes the yearbook.

⁴² Pumping.

⁴³ Places yearbook on the blanket.

⁴⁴ Pumping.

⁴⁵ Picks up the yearbook, and a handful of grapes, and searches for the right page.

⁴⁶ Pumping.

⁴⁷ Wiping grape juice from the yearbook.

⁴⁸ Pumping.

⁴⁹ Rises quickly, holding yearbook.

⁵⁰ Stops pumping.

⁵¹ Embraces the yearbook as though it were the leading lady.

⁵² Barely able to sing because of exhaustion.

⁵³ Crosses a few steps to her, carrying the inflated chair.

⁵⁴ Returns to his pumping, up left.

⁵⁵ Tosses the yearbook on the blanket.

PAUL: Nope. ³³ You said you'd seen the nine o'clock movie.

ANNE: I know. ³⁴ You brought your college yearbook.

PAUL: (Pointing to food.) Go ahead, ³⁵ eat.

ANNE: Tell me. ³⁶ What did you bring?

PAUL: (Sheepishly taking it out of the bag.) My college yearbook.³⁷

ANNE: (Laughing.) Let's see. ³⁸ (Opens it and flips through the pages.) Friedman . . . Friedman . . . hey, you were cute.

PAUL: You're looking at Arthur Friedman. Turn the page.

ANNE: (Does so.) Oh no, ³⁹ is that you? I didn't know you were hydrocephalic.

PAUL: ⁴⁰ Never take a crew cut if you've got a high forehead.

ANNE: (She laughs again at the picture.) ⁴¹ I'll remember.

PAUL: ⁴² I developed late.

ANNE: From what?⁴³

PAUL: ⁴⁴ It's easy for you to talk, Mrs. Miller. We don't have your yearbook here.

ANNE: (She laughs again.) ⁴⁵ Some of us are smart. I'm sorry. You were very . . . interesting-looking.

PAUL: ⁴⁶ Just read under my picture, that's all, smart ass.

ANNE: Paul Friedman. ⁴⁷ President of the Art and Literary Society, I am impressed, treasurer of the Junior Prom, member of the Little Theatre Honor Society, be still my heart . . .

PAUL: Yes, ⁴⁸ ma'am. I played Gaylord Ravenal in *Show Boat.*

ANNE: So did I! ⁴⁹ In girl's camp!

PAUL: I don't believe you.⁵⁰

ANNE: (Sings.)⁵¹

> *You are love*
> *Here in my arms, where you belong . . .*

PAUL: (Singing.)⁵²

> *And here you will stay*
> *I'll not let you away . . .*⁵³

BOTH

> *I want day after day . . .*
> *. . . with you.*

(PAUL stops to hear her baritone.)

PAUL: I think you made a better Gaylord Ravenal than I did.

ANNE: Well, I was probably taller anyway. (Watching him.) You're going to develop quite a bust line.

PAUL: (Pumping even harder.) ⁵⁴ You ought to get Richard to try this.

ANNE: T'ain't funny, ⁵⁵ McGee.

PAUL: I'm sorry.

[56] Brings the inflated chair center stage.

[57] Trying to sit comfortably in the chair, but having difficulty.

[58] Steps back to give Paul more room.

[59] They sit quietly on the blanket, and an awkward moment of silence follows.

[60] They sip wine, hooking elbows in a romantic gesture.

[61] Elbows still entwined.

[62] Slowly untangling their elbows.

[63] Another awkward moment of silence.

[64] Paul takes a deep breath and starts again.

[65] Holds out her glass.

[66] He doesn't see it.

[67] She shakes her glass.

[68] He doesn't hear it.

[69] She taps her glass with a plastic knife. He finally hears it and offers her more wine.

[70] He fills his own glass with wine.

[71] She sips very delicately.

[72] He gulps.

[73] They place the empty glasses on the blanket.

[74] He takes an apple and absently begins to toss it from one hand to another.

(He had finished inflating the chair and now places it for her to sit on.)

[56] Here you are. Ah, I almost forgot the wine. I got a Chablis. You like Chablis?

ANNE: Un-huh.

(PAUL opens the bottle of wine and pours out two glasses. Meanwhile, Anne is struggling to sit comfortably in the inflated chair with no success.)

Well, [57] that's remarkably uncomfortable, isn't it?

PAUL: (Takes chair from her.) There's a trick to it.

ANNE: I hope so.[58]

PAUL: The salesman showed me. First you have to cross your legs.

(PAUL demonstrates how to sit in the chair and falls out of it in a backward somersault.)

(PAUL, disgusted, throws the chair out of the window into the courtyard. He then returns to the blanket and picks up the full wine glasses.)

ANNE: You're quite a demented person, [59] you know?

PAUL: Uh-huh. (Hands her wine glass, she takes it.) [60] To the loveliest leading baritone I know. (They clink glasses and sip.)

ANNE: [61] Did you tell Janet where you were going?

PAUL: No. Did you tell Richard?

ANNE: No.

PAUL: Why not?[62]

ANNE: I don't know. [63] There wasn't time. He was calling long-distance from Cleveland on his way to a client dinner.

PAUL: How is old Richard?[64]

ANNE: [65] Old Richard is very well. He sold his design for a new supermarket.

PAUL: Old Richard is an architect.[66]

ANNE: [67] That's right.

PAUL: What does he design besides supermarkets?[68]

ANNE: Mainly stores, [69] but he has a commission to do a beach house.

PAUL: I'll watch the *Sunday Times Magazine* section.[70]

ANNE: Do. One of the people he's meeting with asked him to design a shopping complex. Not bad, [71] huh?

PAUL: Very complex. [72] Did he tell you about it on the phone?

ANNE: Yes.[73]

PAUL: Oh, [74] I see. That's why you didn't have time to tell him.

[75] He accidentally tosses the apple into Anne's lap and starts to reach for it.

[76] She stops him with a warning finger and places the apple on the blanket.

[77] She rises, still munching on a chicken leg, and slowly backs upstage until stopped by the radiator.

[78] Paul tries to find a more comfortable position on the blanket.

[79] Anne sits on the radiator.

[80] Quickly rises.

[81] He walks to her on his hands and knees and then sits next to her on the radiator.

[82] Drops the chicken leg.

[83] Staring at the chicken leg.

[84] Quickly crosses down left and addresses an unseen Judge, just above the heads of the audience.

ANNE: (Coolly.) Your turn.

PAUL: [75] Janet was making paella. Have you ever made it?

ANNE: No.[76]

(They look at each other.)

PAUL: Well, the trick in making a really superior paella is to get the chicken to brown and the clams to steam and the sausages to fry at the same time so they can be added to the rice at just the proper moment. Otherwise you get soggy rice. Then, too, overcooking can turn the golden yellow of saffron rice a warm beige, which although pleasing to look at is not a sign of really superior rice at our house.

(ANNE gives him a knowing look, which he sees.)

She was not to be disturbed.

ANNE: A likely story.

PAUL: Every bit as likely as yours.

ANNE: (She has taken a chicken leg, now she stops eating it.) [77] I think I'm feeling a little self-conscious. I just forgot how to swallow.

PAUL: (He has taken a bite of his sandwich.) Close your mouth and push.

(Beat.)

[78] I feel pretty self-conscious myself.

ANNE: Why didn't we tell them? [79] It would have been so simple.

PAUL: Sure it would. [80] "Hey, Janet, old liberated thing. I met this girl at the apartment you sent me to look at and we got to talking and she's a lot of laughs so I asked her out to dinner. Janet, stop crying in the paella. You're making it salty." Want a banana?

ANNE: No, thanks.

PAUL: How about an orange?[81]

ANNE: Okay. (He hands her one.) So we didn't tell them. Where's the harm?

PAUL: None at all. Of course, if they catch us it's headlines in the *West Side News.*

ANNE: Isn't this absurd.

PAUL: Absolutely.

ANNE: [82] I feel so guilty.

PAUL: Me, [83] too.

ANNE: (In a fake lawyer's voice.) [84] And do you seriously expect the jury to believe, Mr. Friedman, that you and Mrs. Miller ate fruit salad and read comic books while on the floor of the aforementioned love nest?

[85] Quickly crosses down right to addesss the same Judge.

[86] Crosses down center.

[87] Crosses down center.

[88] Faces Paul.

[89] Faces Anne. Their lips almost touch, but he spins to address the Judge.

[90] He turns back to her.

[91] She turns to address the Judge.

[92] Crosses down right.

[93] Walks over the blanket to get her shoes, stepping on the fruit.

[94] Anne has her back to Paul, removing the crushed fruit from her toes.

[95] Crosses slowly to her.

[96] Turns to face him, still holding the crushed fruit in her hands, and then quickly turns away.

[97] Paul pulls Anne to the door and makes her shake hands with "Janet."

[98] Anne bows to her left to indicate "Richard."

[99] Paul vigorously shakes "Richard's" hand.

PAUL: Objection! [85] I move that the last remark be stricken from the record, your honor.

ANNE: [86] Objection sustained. While on the floor of this aforementioned apartment?

PAUL: I do, [87] your honor. I further testify that at no time during our tryst . . .

ANNE: Objection.[88]

PAUL: Assignation . . .[89]

ANNE: Objection.

PAUL: [90] Encounter? (She makes no objection.) At no time during our encounter did Mrs. Miller ever lay a glove on me.

ANNE: (With sudden seriousness.) My God, [91] we're having a brief encounter. Strike that from the record.

PAUL: (Picking up her mood.) You want to go, [92] don't you?

ANNE: (Getting on her shoes.) Yes, [93] I think so.

PAUL: You know how silly that is?

ANNE: Uh-huh.[94]

PAUL: I mean, [95] if Richard and Janet were here there'd be nothing wrong with it, would there?

ANNE: (Getting her coat.) Hardly.[96]

PAUL: So? Nothing's happening they couldn't see. What's the problem?

ANNE: Paul, they're *not* here.

PAUL: (Gets up, runs to door and opens it.) Janet! [97] Come on in! Plop yourself down. I'd like you to meet Anne. Anne, Janet.
(*Anne* whirls around, then realizes he's playing.)
She says she thinks you're awfully attractive.

ANNE: I think you're nuts.

PAUL: Janet?

ANNE: No, you.

PAUL: Oh. Haven't you forgotten something?

ANNE: What?

PAUL: You didn't introduce me to Richard.

ANNE: Oh, [98] what the hell. Richard, this is my old friend, Paul Friedman. Paul and I were in *Show Boat* together. Richard says, "How are you, old man?"

PAUL: In the pink, [99] buddy. In the pink. Had a little hernia trouble a while back, but everything's okay now.

ANNE: Richard says you looked like you might have had a little hernia trouble.

PAUL: Thanks, pal. Golly, Dick, you sure do sit up straight.

ANNE: Well, if it comes to that, what about Janet?

[100] Paul opens the door again.

[101] They wave "good-bye" to both "Janet" and "Richard."

[102] Paul puts his hand around Anne's waist and leads her gently toward the blanket center stage, as the curtain falls.

PAUL: Yeah, we're very proud of Janet's vertebrae at our house. Well, [100] Janet has to go.

ANNE: I hope it's nothing Richard said.

PAUL: No, her group is sitting in at the George Washington Bridge until they build a Martha Washington Bridge. But she wants the three of us to stay and enjoy ourselves.

ANNE: That's very sweet.

PAUL: Aw, [101] Richard has to go, too. He's designing poodle pissoirs for the East Side. Bye, Dick.

ANNE: (Sourly.) Nice meeting you, Janet.

PAUL: (Closes door.) [102] Alone at last.

FROM

Requiem for Romance (1979)
by LUCY WALKER

The most recent play in the collection of modern scenes, this drama focuses on an unconventional black family in the South who painfully become aware of their own inadequacy and sense of disillusionment through a series of domestic mishaps. The title of the drama also suggests the mournful "hymn" that each member of the family sings as the struggle to realize personal goals and dreams is met with further frustration, despair, and eventual collapse.

The plot revolves around the eccentric Plum family, a collection of social misfits, rebels, fanatics, and dreamers who seek refuge from the outside world in the comforting lies they tell one another and who mirror their own frustration in the "games" they play with one another.

They have gathered to celebrate the homecoming of Lena Whiteman, the eldest daughter, who has achieved a measure of success by earning a college degree from a Northern university. The mood is not as happy as anticipated, however, because there is obvious resentment and jealousy from Juke, the alcoholic eldest son, and from the increasingly rebellious and unpredictable Romance, a younger son.

Even Lena is subdued and withdrawn when she arrives, and it becomes known that she and her mother, the stern and unbending Reba, have never actually understood or even liked each other. Against this cold and apparently uncaring family atmosphere, the tragic events of the play unfold: Romance, in a fit of rage, kills his older brother and must be taken away to a mental institution.

In playing the scene, which immediately follows the shooting of Juke, the actors should capture the disbelief and horror that has resulted from such a senseless act. It is also necessary to suggest the progressively insane nature of Romance, particularly as he drifts between the "make-believe" world of his childhood and the harsh reality of his present deed.

The other characters in the scene, especially Reba, are so overcome with grief and guilt that they cannot comprehend the situation. There is also a mood of fear of what will happen to Romance when he is committed to the mental institution.

Cast:

> Holly
> Reba
> Romance
> Lena

Scene:

> A shabby living room furnished with odds and ends, whatnots, and pictures of Jesus Christ, Gospel singers, and crosses. It is Sunday afternoon.

ACT II

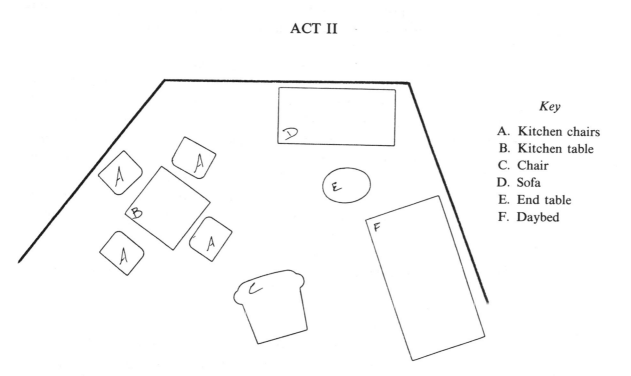

Key

A. Kitchen chairs
B. Kitchen table
C. Chair
D. Sofa
E. End table
F. Daybed

As the scene opens, Holly, a white policeman, leads Romance in from the dining room. Romance is wrapped in a straitjacket and seems unaware of what has just happened. There is uneasiness and tension in the air as he suddenly realizes that he cannot move his arms. He begins to cry as his mother rushes to comfort him.

The mood swiftly changes from sympathy to anger, however, and his mother assumes the burden of guilt for Romance's actions; he is completely isolated in thought and dream, breaking silence only to utter curses or threats. Every attempt to reach out to him or comfort him is met with rejection.

As the scene opens Reba is seated in the chair, down center. Lena is sitting on the daybed facing her. Holly has Romance by the arm of a straitjacket, standing down right.

[1] Trying to free himself.

[2] Unable to look at Romance.

[3] Frees himself but does not move.

[4] Rises and crosses to him, placing her hand on his shoulder.

[5] Rushes to Reba, falls on his knees, and places his head in her lap.

[6] Pats his head, as she looks upward.

[7] Inches closer to her.

[8] Crosses to Reba, kneels with one arm around her shoulder and one arm on Romance.

[9] Crosses up right by crawling on his knees.

[10] Crosses on knees down left, and pleads with Lena.

[11] Crosses on knees to Reba, who is center.

[12] Rises, with Holly's help.

[13] Collapses on the floor and kicks like a child.

[14] Curls up on the floor.

[15] Lena crosses to Romance and lies on the floor beside him, trying to comfort him.

[16] Reba crosses slowly to the daybed, on the brink of collapse.

[17] Raises his head.

[18] Kneels to pray, facing center.

[19] Sits up with Lena's help.

HOLLY: Go. Move it, [1] Romance.

REBA: My son! [2] What have they done ta you? You gotta take him 'way in this thang?

HOLLY: We can't chance him harming anyone else, Reba.

ROMANCE: RELEASE ME! [3] It's time to pump blood out into the many little veins that help me fly.

LENA: Juke is dead, [4] Romance.

ROMANCE: Get away from me! [5] Get thee to a convention! The devil knows no pain. Help me, Mama!
(Cries in his Mama's arms.)

REBA: God! [6] You listen' ta me? You hear me talkin' ta you?

ROMANCE: He don't exist. [7] He can't exist. It's a lie!

REBA: My oldest son, Lord. He was leavin' with his little baby tonight. Maybe he coulda made it. Only you know that. Lord, I just want you ta know that I loved my sons, and I woulda never killed my boys no matter what I threatened.

HOLLY: Reba, [8] please.

REBA: Lemme be, Richard! I just wish I knew why, Lord. Are you testin' me, like ya tested Job? I'm weak in my flesh, Lord, and can't hardly walk no more. Please help me hold on. My soul's bein' ripped apart, Lord. And I don't know why.

ROMANCE: They coming for me, ain't they? [9] They'll never take me alive. I'm on Self-Destruct! [10] Get me out of this thing, Lena. Mama . . . [11] I . . . I don't . . . Please!

REBA: Don't look at me like that! [12] After what you done. God, you are and forever was his keeper. Take him to your bosom and rock him, Lord.

ROMANCE: Mama! Don't do this to me. Help me!

REBA: This shoulda been a celebration, not a time to hang funeral wreaths and wear black suits and dresses.

ROMANCE: I won't do it anymore. Punish me, [13] Mama! Beat me with the rubber hose or the broom handle, but don't send me to that place again! They'll force me to take little green and pink pills that make me think. I can't do that. [14] I can't take time to think about the bruises. Mama, [15] please don't do this to me. I love you more than ever, [16] Mama.

HOLLY: It's time to go now, boy. Ain't nothing your Mama can do.

ROMANCE: I love you the MOST, [17] Mama!

REBA: You're sick, [18] and I can't help ya no more! I can't cover up no more. Never no more!

ROMANCE: I got to be near you, [19] Mama. I need you! Smoke's

[20] Reba crosses a few steps toward Romance.

[21] Reba kneels beside Romance.

[22] Hugs Romance, while facing Holly.

[23] Lena and Holly help Romance to his feet.

[24] His legs collapse for a moment, and he almost falls.

[25] Rises and leans on the daybed for support.

[26] Shakes Romance rather roughly.

[27] With deadly calm, Romance crosses down center. Lena follows with her hand on his arm.

[28] Starts to lead Romance off, up right.

choking me, Mama. [20] The house is on fire! Don't leave me alone, Mama!

REBA: Dear God in Heaven! What's happenin' ta my family?

ROMANCE: Please, Mama. I won't embarrass you no more.

HOLLY: [21] It's time to go now.

ROMANCE: You knew I was scared, Mama. Why didn't you help me?

HOLLY: You're upsetting your mother, boy!

LENA: Leave him alone, [22] Richard. Let him get it all out.

REBA: Git up an' face it like a man, and maybe God will see fit to help ya.

ROMANCE: You have to help me, Mama! It's Sunday. Don't let them take me away on a Sunday. I didn't even go to church today.

REBA: It ain't a Sunday yet. But ask the Lord for mercy anyway. He'll help ya.

ROMANCE: I'd rather be killed. These memories, they hurt bad, Mama.

(He starts to cry again.)

REBA: You in the Lord's hands now, boy. You been snatched away from my protectin' arms.

ROMANCE: I can't go back there, [23] Mama! I don't want to talk to strangers, and tell them our secrets. My past. [24] They want to know, Mama! They can see the scars. They want to dig up the headless bodies. They tampering with my memories. I can't . . . Smoke stings inside my head!

REBA: [25] People was scared ta come because a ya. Nobody came. Nobody! I bought a new dress. Cook'd fur three days. An' the girls even disappear'd.

HOLLY: [26] My partner is getting impatient out there. Stand on your own or I'll let you fall on your face.

LENA: You'll want me to come, Richard.

HOLLY: Perhaps you should stay with your mother.

LENA: She'll be alright.

REBA: Nobody came. Nobody! Good thing. They miss'd a murder.

ROMANCE: Officer, [27] I'm not insane. It's . . . you see, it started when I was sixteen. The house burned down and I got this fluttering inside my head. It's like a butterfly hatched out of his cocoon. A free-flying, red butterfly screaming for freedom. Trying to eat my head off from the inside.

HOLLY: I gave you a chance, [28] boy . . . and you . . . Oh, come on!

[29] Lena and Holly each take one of Romance's arms.

[30] Reba slowly sinks on the daybed.

[31] Raises her head heavenward.

[32] Buries her head in a pillow on the daybed, as the scene quietly concludes.

ROMANCE: (Gives an animal scream.) [29] Ahhhheeee!

REBA: It fell apart! [30] I can't keep nothin' anymore. Everthin' ran away from me. Ah, my legs hurt.

HOLLY: Reba! (She doesn't hear.) Give the station a call first thing Monday morning, Lena. And take care of Reba.

LENA: I'm coming with you. Come on, Romance.

ROMANCE: It started when . . . I had vibrations inside my head. [31] The doctors said I had sinus. Doctors don't know nothing. Who's that? I don't know him, Lena.

REBA: They have him now. Ain't no more I can do fur him. I failed. I tried. God knows I tried. It was too many. I'm sorry . . . I'm sorry.

ROMANCE: (Screams offstage.) [32] Mammmmmmmmmmah!

Act III
ON PLAYING AVANT GARDE SCENES

It has often been said, perhaps as an apology, that it is easier for the beginning actor to understand the action and meaning of avant garde plays by not thinking too much, that the best style of performance is improvisational, or spontaneous reaction to the environment or the situation.

Although there is much truth in both of these suggestions, it is possible for the beginning actor to come to terms with the difficulty of playing avant garde scenes if the following principles are explored in carefully observed and orchestrated rehearsals.

First, avant garde plays seem to distort the appearance of reality in a variety of ways. The distortion may take several avenues of approach, but it usually begins with the character's loss of human qualities, so that what emerges is a machinelike, almost dehumanized individual who has no sense of direction or purpose in life.

Second, lacking an identity and personality, avant garde characters seem to have no sense of time or tempo and may often seem to despair of life itself. In their melancholy moments they seek, usually in vain, to discover who they are and more often than not are reduced to a series of nervous, meaningless impulses or responses that prove their essential worthlessness.

Third, avant garde plays are peopled with characters who treat one another with apparently deliberate cruelty and aggressive hostility, even though admitting to themselves that existing alone is far worse than living together with another human being. Isolated in vague and featureless environments, these frustrated individuals strike out against society in barely audible cries and plead for some meaning and order for their lives.

Fourth, such "absurd" plays demand an ingenious, or sometimes offbeat approach to characterization and performance in order to highlight the futility and despair these "loners" feel in living a life that seemingly has no purpose.

Some examples of this approach to characterization for avant garde plays might include extremely fast or unduly slow movement to emphasize the urgency or the futility of a given moment; mechanical speech like that of a robot to suggest the loss of individuality or humanity; and exaggerated poses, portrait or comic-book caricatures, conflicting postures, and incongruous facial expressions that help to distort and contradict the meaning of the words spoken and the actions performed in a given situation.

Similarly, avant garde plays often demand a background of sound effects, unusual hand

85

props, slides or projections, symbolic signs, mime and dance to help confuse the true meaning of the words and actions.

Some examples of these performance aids that help to reinforce the absurdity of the situation might include the loud beating of a heart played on tape as two characters discuss the meaning of life; cubes or prisms suspended from the ceiling, or slides projected on a screen at the rear of the performance area, to suggest the vacuum created by a life that has no meaning; masks or burlesquelike mime to disguise a character's true feelings; and signs or placards with painted question marks and exclamation points placed about the playing area to draw audience attention to moments in which thoughts or actions of some significance are to be expressed.

Regardless of the approach taken, avant garde plays direct the audience to think, and the actor should use the opportunity to appear sensible and ordinary no matter what the situation or the indicated behavior.

To generalize convincingly is the primary goal in avant garde performance, not to appear merely foolish or silly. Allow the script to suggest the laughable by the actions performed, and concentrate on mirroring the terror and fear that accompany these lost and abandoned characters in search of their identity.

Each of the selected scenes, although not all typically "absurd" in the exaggerated sense, share a common avant garde impulse: the characters are desperately in search of understanding and compassion from another human being. The selections range from the almost realistic *Zoo Story* and *The Runner Stumbles* to the thought-provoking *Wandering* and *Lemonade,* and each requires a sensitive and perceptive approach to highlight the intent.

Zoo Story, for example, should be played as naturally as possible; it is only the situation that is absurd. The characters begin as average men who happen to meet on a park bench. As they exchange polite conversation, however, it becomes apparent that they are playing roles and that beneath their rather normal exterior is a vicious, animalistic instinct that feeds on violence. The actors should approach the playing of the scene like two seasoned boxers who test each other in the opening rounds of the fight before closing in to deliver the knockout blow.

The same approach could also be used for *The Runner Stumbles,* although here the actors should recall that the play is a flashback and that the characters are recalling and reliving events that have already taken place. While the basic approach to playing the scene is realistic, there should be a dreamlike quality to the movement and the speech, especially as the characters drift from one realm of thought to another. Remember, also, that this scene encourages direct address to the audience to reveal inner thoughts of the characters and actually places imaginary characters in the audience's down-stage seating area.

Both *Wandering* and *Lemonade* allow for more innovation and creativity in staging and performance, and should be complemented with sound effects, music or projections, exaggerated props, and suggestive costumes that might provoke the audience to think. A good approach is to set the scene in an empty playing area, with little detail of a specific environment, and then to fill the space with objects, set pieces, or signs that eventually reveal the locale. The characters should also appear to be isolated in a vast emptiness with their first entrance and should suggest definite, exaggerated types of comic personalities that could also have been found in the period scenes of Act I.

FROM

The Zoo Story (1960)
by EDWARD ALBEE

For all its cruelty and violence, this avant garde play is supposedly concerned with the religious pilgrimage of two emotionally and spiritually crippled men who happen to meet on a Sunday afternoon in late summer. As they sit on a park bench surrounded by the inviting view of Central Park, the characters engage in the symbolic ritual of first introducing themselves, then sharing a series of amusing personal anecdotes, and eventually acquainting themselves with each other.

Slowly, however, the conversation takes a more serious turn, and both men reveal themselves as disillusioned, tormented misfits apparently resigned to a boring life that has no value or meaning. As the tone of the exchanges becomes more heated and threatening, the men become more animalistic and protective of their territory, until, at last, one is killed in a knife fight.

The title of the play also suggests the narrow world view that each character holds as a result of his own life experience, and it is possible to understand each man's sense of isolation and despair in terms of the social pressures and demands that have encaged them like animals on public display at the zoo.

Peter, a man in his early forties, is obviously a representative of the upper middle class. He wears a tweed suit, smokes a pipe, and carries horn-rimmed glasses. He is sophisticated and well educated, a fact he frequently points out with pride. Jerry, a man in his late thirties, is carelessly dressed and evidently dependent on others for his livelihood. He is despondent and moody, and his anger rises at the slightest provocation or minor mishap.

In playing the scene, the actors should recall that each of the characters has a secret that he does not wish to reveal. To protect his individuality and sense of independence, each man plays games with the other, taking care not to allow any intrusion into matters that are personal or private. The game continues for some time, until Jerry tires of it and asserts himself in a physical, violent manner.

There should be a suggestion in the scene that the men are not so different from each other in attitude or mentality, and that they may well be dual characters, each reflecting a different side of the other. This can be suggested if the actors assume similar positions at times, use similar gestures or facial expressions, or suggest similar vocal patterns of expression.

Special care should be taken to suggest to the audience that Jerry is consciously enacting a ritual, a pattern of repetitive insults and physical abuses, that will provoke Peter to do what is necessary to end the suffering and pain he imagines himself experiencing. There

Zoo Story

should also be a sense of urgency and desperation in Jerry's movement and pleading speech so that the audience senses that the time is quickly passing for the desired response of Peter.

Cast:

    Jerry

    Peter

Scene:

    Central Park, on a Sunday afternoon in summer. The present.

ACT I

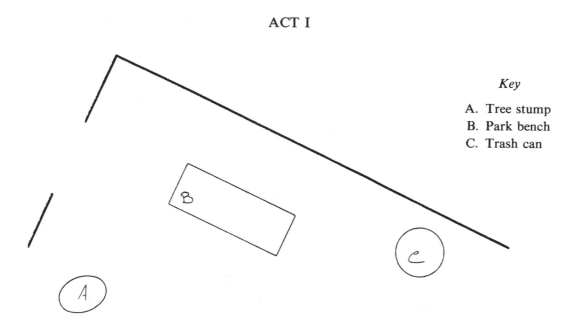

Key

A. Tree stump
B. Park bench
C. Trash can

As the scene opens, Peter is seated on his bench reading a book. He stops, cleans his glasses, and stares off into space. Occasionally he takes a bite of a sandwich or an apple that he carries in a brown paper bag.

Jerry, unshaven and wearing wrinkled clothing, enters cautiously and slowly starts to approach Peter, appearing as if he might attack from behind. His movement is hesitant and halting, and he glances over his shoulder frequently to see if anyone is following him.

Just as Jerry is close enough to tap Peter on the shoulder, Peter turns quickly around and is startled to see a wild-eyed, frantic young man pointing at him. They remain frozen for a moment, each afraid of what the other might do.

As the scene begins, Jerry is seated on the extreme left of the bench, and Peter is huddled next to him.

1 Playing hide and-seek between two of his fingers.

2 Folding his Sunday newspaper very neatly.

3 Doing very deep breathing exercises, which continue audibly.

4 Opening his attaché case, on the right, to put the newspaper away.

5 Flipping one latch closed rather loudly, Peter halts.

JERRY: (mysteriously) Peter, 1 do you want to know what happened at the zoo?

PETER: Ah, ha, ha. The what? Oh, yes; the zoo. Oh, ho, ho. Well, 2 I had my own zoo there for a moment with . . . hee, hee, the parakeets getting dinner ready, and the . . . ha, ha, whatever it was, the . . .

JERRY: (calmly) Yes, 3 that was very funny, Peter. I wouldn't have expected it. But do you want to hear about what happened at the zoo, or not?

PETER: Yes. Yes, by all means; 4 tell me what happened at the zoo. Oh, my. I don't know what happened to me.

JERRY: Now I'll let you in on what happened at the zoo; but first, 5 I should tell you why I went to the zoo. I went to the zoo to find out more about the way people exist with animals,

⁶ Peter flips the other latch rather loudly, and halts.

⁷ Peter slides to the right slightly, and places his attaché case between himself and Jerry to use as an armrest.

⁸ Checking his sleeve for dirt.

⁹ Staring off into space.

¹⁰ Discreetly brushing off his sleeve, Peter turns away.

¹¹ Places the attaché case flat on the bench to separate himself as much as possible from Jerry.

¹² Releasing the last of his exercise breaths.

¹⁸ Shoves the attaché case to the ground.

¹⁴ Grabs his throbbing arm.

¹⁵ Turns his back to Jerry.

¹⁶ Gets on his knees behind Peter and grabs him around the neck with one arm, pointing off down right with the other arm.

¹⁷ Slowly frees himself and retreats to the end of the bench, left.

and the way animals exist with each other, and with people too.

⁶ It probably wasn't a fair test, what with everyone separated by bars from everybody else, the animals for the most part from each other, and always the people from the animals. But, ⁷ if it's a zoo, that's the way it is. (He pokes PETER on the arm.) Move over.

PETER: (friendly) I'm sorry, ⁸ haven't you enough room? (He shifts a little.)

JERRY: (smiling slightly) Well, ⁹ all the animals are there, and all the people are there, and it's Sunday and all the children are there. (He pokes PETER again.) Move over.

PETER: (patiently, still friendly) All right. (He moves some more, and JERRY has all the room he might need.)

JERRY: And it's a hot day, ¹⁰ so all the stench is there, too, and all the balloon sellers, and all the ice cream sellers, and all the seals are barking, and all the birds are screaming. (Pokes PETER harder.) Move over!

PETER: (beginning to be annoyed) Look here, ¹¹ you have more than enough room! (But he moves more, and is now fairly cramped at one end of the bench.)

JERRY: And I am there, and it's feeding time at the lion's house, and the lion keeper comes into the lion cage, one of the lion cages, to feed one of the lions. ¹² (Punches PETER on the arm, hard.) MOVE OVER!

PETER: (very annoyed) I can't move over any more, and stop hitting me. What's the matter with you?

JERRY: ¹³ Do you want to hear the story? (Punches PETER's arm again.)

PETER: (flabbergasted) I'm not so sure! I certainly don't want to be punched in the arm.

JERRY: (punches PETER's arm again) Like that?

PETER: Stop it! ¹⁴ What's the matter with you?

JERRY: I'm crazy, you bastard.

PETER: That isn't funny.¹⁵

JERRY: Listen to me, ¹⁶ Peter. I want this bench. You go sit on the bench over there, and if you're good I'll tcll you the rest of the story.

PETER: (flustered) But ¹⁷ . . . whatever for? What *is* the matter with you? Besides, I see no reason why I should give up this bench. I sit on this bench almost every Sunday afternoon, in

[18] Rises on the bench and hovers over Peter.

[19] Sits on the back of the bench, with his feet resting on the seat.

[20] Still holding his injured arm, but trying to be conversational.

[21] Stands on the seat.

[22] Laughs louder.

[23] Waves his finger in a threatening manner.

[24] Jerry grabs his finger and begins to twist it .

[25] Peter screams in pain, but cannot free himself.

[26] Slowly sinking to a sitting position next to Peter.

[27] Finally removing his finger with a painful jerk.

[28] Grips the seat with both of his hands, and locks himself in position with his eyes tightly closed.

[29] Opens his eyes in surprise at the sound.

[30] Grabs the seat even tighter.

[31] Reaches for the attaché case and then suddenly leaps up on the seat, where he swings the case back and forth like a gorilla. At the conclusion of his speech, Jerry tosses the attaché case in the trash can, up stage.

[32] Slowly turning full circle on the seat of the bench.

good weather. It's secluded here; there's never anyone sitting here, so I have it all to myself.

JERRY: (softly) Get off this bench, [18] Peter; I want it.

PETER: (almost whining) No.

JERRY: [19] I said I want this bench, and I'm going to have it. Now get over there.

PETER: People can't have everything they want. [20] You should know that; it's a rule; people can have some of the things they want, but they can't have everything.

JERRY: (laughs) Imbecile! [21] You're slow-witted!

PETER: Stop that!

JERRY: [22] You're a vegetable! Go lie on the ground.

PETER: (intense) Now *you* listen to me. [23] I've put up with you all afternoon.

JERRY: [24] Not really.

PETER: [25] LONG ENOUGH. I've put up with you long enough. I've listened to you because you seemed . . . well, because I thought you wanted to talk to somebody.

JERRY: You put things well; [26] economically, and yet . . . oh, what is the word I want to put justice to your . . . JESUS, you make me sick . . . get off here and give me my bench!

PETER: [27] MY BENCH!

JERRY: (pushes PETER almost, but not quite, off the bench) Get out of my sight.

PETER: (regaining his position) God da . . . mn you. [28] That's enough! I've had enough of you. I will not give up this bench; you can't have it, and that's that. Now, go away.

(JERRY snorts but does not move.)[29]

Go away, I said.

(JERRY does not move.)

[30] Get away from here. If you don't move on . . . you're a bum . . . that's what you are . . . If you don't move on, I'll get a policeman here and make you go.

(JERRY laughs, stays.)

I warn you, I'll call a policeman.

JERRY: (softly) [31] You won't find a policeman around here; they're all over on the west side of the park chasing fairies down from trees or out of the bushes. That's all they do. That's their function. So scream your head off; it won't do you any good.

PETER: POLICE! I warn you, I'll have you arrested. POLICE! (Pause) I said POLICE! (Pause) I feel ridiculous.

JERRY: [32] You look ridiculous: a grown man screaming for the

³³ Looking sadly toward the trash can.

³⁴ Crouches in an animallike position and whispers in Peter's ear.

³⁵ Turns to face him; their noses actually touch.

³⁶ Stands on seat of the bench.

³⁷ Takes a few steps backward, and then halts.

³⁸ Sits on the back of the bench and folds his arms.

³⁹ Reaches over and plucks the handkerchief from Peter's suit pocket. He snaps the handkerchief open and spreads it over his upturned face.

⁴⁰ Quickly and quietly retrieves his attaché case and returns to his seat.

⁴¹ He gestures to the sky, but the handkerchief still covers his face.

⁴² Hugging his attaché case to his chest.

⁴³ Slowly removes the handkerchief and leans menacingly toward Peter.

⁴⁴ Spreading the handkerchief on the back of the bench, ready to begin combat.

police on a bright Sunday afternoon in the park with nobody harming you. If a policeman *did* fill his quota and come sludging over this way he'd probably take you in as a nut.

PETER: (with disgust and impotence) Great God, ³³ I just came here to read, and now you want me to give up the bench. You're mad.

JERRY: Hey, ³⁴ I got news for you, as they say. I'm on your precious bench, and you're never going to have it for yourself again.

PETER: (furious) Look, ³⁵ you; get off my bench. I don't care if it makes any sense or not. I want this bench to myself; I want you OFF IT!

JERRY: (mocking) Aw ³⁶ . . . look who's mad.

PETER: ³⁷ GET OFF!

JERRY: ³⁸ Do you know how ridiculous you look *now?*

PETER: (His fury and self-consciousness have possessed him) It doesn't matter. (He is almost crying) GET AWAY FROM MY BENCH!

JERRY: Why? ³⁹ You have everything in the world you want; you've told me about your home, and your family, and *your own* little zoo. You have everything, and now you want this bench. Are these the things men fight for? Tell me, Peter, is this bench, this iron and this wood, is this your honor? Is this the thing in the world you'd fight for? Can you think of anything more absurd?

PETER: Absurd? Look, ⁴⁰ I'm not going to talk to you about honor, or even try to explain it to you. Besides, it isn't a question of honor; but even if it were, you wouldn't understand.

JERRY: (contemptuously) ⁴¹ You don't even know what you're saying, do you? This is probably the first time in your life you've had anything more trying to face than changing your cats' toilet box. Stupid! Don't you have any idea, not even the slightest, what other people *need?*

PETER: Oh, ⁴² boy, listen to you; well, you don't need this bench. That's for sure.

JERRY: Yes; yes, ⁴³ I do.

PETER: (quivering) I've come here for years; I have hours of great pleasure, great satisfaction, right here. And that's important to a man. I'm a responsible person, and I'm a GROWNUP. This is my bench, and you have no right to take it away from me.

JERRY: Fight for it, then, Defend yourself; ⁴⁴ defend your bench.

PETER: You've *pushed* me to it. Get up and fight.

[45] Peter lunges for the handkerchief, but Jerry is too fast and snatches it away.

[46] Sets the attaché case to the side, right.

[47] Tickles Peter's face with the handkerchief.

[48] Grabs for the handkerchief again, but Jerry pulls it away.

[49] Stuffs the handkerchief in Peter's suit pocket.

[50] Jumps down from the bench, walks several steps down left, and then turns dramatically as he throws the knife toward Peter.

[51] Moves quickly to Peter and pulls him from the bench by his tie.

[52] Backing away toward the tree stump stage right.

[53] With each slap, Peter retreats one step until he is finally pushed down on the stump by Jerry at the conclusion of the speech.

[54] Peter moves to bench, left, and Jerry places his foot on the stump and his hand on his chin in the pose of Rodin's "The Thinker."

JERRY: Like a man?

PETER: (still angry) Yes, like a man, if you insist on mocking me even further.[45]

JERRY: I'll have to give you credit for one thing: you *are* a vegetable, and a slightly nearsighted one, I think . . .

PETER: [46] THAT'S ENOUGH . . .

JERRY: . . . but, [47] you know, as they say on TV all the time— you know—and I mean this, Peter, you have a certain dignity; it surprises me . . .

PETER: STOP![48]

JERRY: (rises lazily) Very well, [49] Peter, we'll battle for the bench, but we're not evenly matched.

(He takes out and clicks open an ugly-looking knife.)

PETER: (suddenly awakening to the reality of the situation) You *are* mad! You're stark raving mad! YOU'RE GOING TO KILL ME!

(But before PETER has time to think what to do, JERRY tosses the knife at PETER's feet.)

JERRY: [50] There you go. Pick it up. You have the knife and we'll be more evenly matched.

PETER: (horrified) No!

JERRY: (rushes over to PETER, grabs him by the collar; PETER rises; their faces almost touch) [51] Now you pick up that knife and you fight with me. You fight for your self-respect; you fight for that goddamned bench.

PETER: (struggling) No! Let [52] . . . let go of me! He . . . Help!

JERRY: (slaps PETER on each "fight") You fight, you miserable bastard; fight for that bench; fight for your parakeets; fight for your cats; fight for your two daughters; fight for your wife; fight for your manhood, you pathetic little vegetable. (Spits in PETER's face) [53] You couldn't even get your wife with a male child.

PETER: (breaks away, enraged) It's a matter of genetics, [54] not manhood, you . . . you monster.

(He darts down, picks up the knife and backs off a little; he is breathing heavily.)

I'll give you one last chance; get out of here and leave me alone!

(He holds the knife with a firm arm, but far in front of him, not to attack but to defend.)

JERRY: (sighs heavily) So be it!

(With a rush he charges PETER and impales himself on the knife. Tableau: For just a moment, complete silence,

⁵⁵ Looking in all directions for help.

⁵⁶ Jerry extends his hand toward Peter, and then quietly lowers his head. Peter stands still for a moment, and then slowly backs away as the scene concludes.

JERRY impaled on the knife at the end of PETER's still firm arm. Then PETER screams, pulls away, leaving the knife in JERRY. JERRY is motionless, on point. Then he, too, screams, and it must be the sound of an infuriated and fatally wounded animal. With the knife in him, he stumbles back to the bench that PETER had vacated. He crumbles there, sitting facing PETER, his eyes wide in agony, his mouth open.)

PETER: (whispering) Oh my God, ⁵⁵ oh my God, oh my God . . . (He repeats these words many times, very rapidly.)

JERRY: (JERRY is dying; but now his expression seems to change. His features relax, and while his voice varies, sometimes wrenched with pain, for the most part he seems removed from his dying. He smiles.)

Thank you, Peter. I mean that, now; thank you very much. (PETER's mouth drops open. He cannot move; he is transfixed.)

Oh, ⁵⁶ Peter, I was so afraid I'd drive you away.

FROM

Wandering (1966)
by LANFORD WILSON

The essential seriousness of this avant garde play is hidden in its almost cartoonlike approach to describing the vivid episodes of a young man's life as he moves from adolescence to maturity. As the title suggests, the young man is aimless and uncertain as he wanders from one attraction to another; but there is also the suggestion that his travels result in meaning and purpose as he becomes aware of the many directions life may take if only one chooses the right path.

In playing the scene, it is clearly important that the behavior of the characters be simple and free from exaggeration. The actors should also retire to the "Attention" position when not speaking and should face the audience in the presentational style of delivery whenever possible.

Actions and props should be pantomimed, and the scene should be performed rather rapidly, with the performers changing roles as quickly and as obviously as the script indicates. The only pauses in the action are noted in the author's stage directions, and the desired effect is to move easily from one episode to another without any apparent separation in the events he has experienced.

There should be a minimum of set pieces or staging devices, and the performers are encouraged to suggest the many changes of locale within the scene by rotating a single

Wandering

bench or chair so that it symbolizes the different environments called for in the script.

For purposes of smooth transition, a description of the suggested environments in which the action takes place is included for performance consideration. There are also included some hints for the many changes of character necessary to suggest the variety of people with whom the young man comes in contact during his wandering. Because these individuals are part of the young man's imagination, they may be played with more freedom of expression and may even look like puppets or buffoons in preposterous or absurdly exaggerated costumes.

A suggestion for movement in the scene is circular, so that the audience may visualize the recurring pattern of the young man's travels and also sense that each episode ultimately returns him to his starting point. The decidedly military nature of the script might even suggest that movement is done in a "march" fashion, or that the imaginary individuals who appear and disappear so rapidly are merely nightmarish phantoms who constantly interrupt the young man's dreams and lead him on to the next episode.

Cast:

> He
> She
> Him

Scene:

> The present. The past. The future.

ACT I

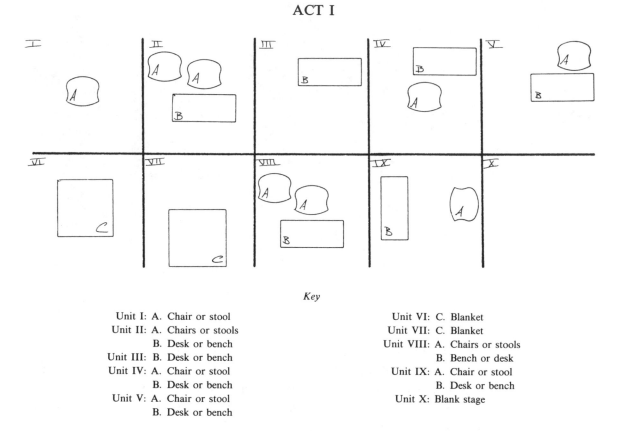

Key

Unit I: A. Chair or stool	Unit VI: C. Blanket
Unit II: A. Chairs or stools	Unit VII: C. Blanket
B. Desk or bench	Unit VIII: A. Chairs or stools
Unit III: B. Desk or bench	B. Bench or desk
Unit IV: A. Chair or stool	Unit IX: A. Chair or stool
B. Desk or bench	B. Desk or bench
Unit V: A. Chair or stool	Unit X: Blank stage
B. Desk or bench	

SUGGESTED LOCALES

UNIT I: A Living Room.

Him is the young son, He is the angry Father, and She is the disappointed Mother. He is right of the chair facing left; She is left of the chair facing right; and Him is seated in the chair centerstage.

UNIT II: A Business Office.

He is the gruff-voiced employer, She is the gum-chewing secretary, and Him is the nervous job applicant. He sits in a chair with his feet upon the desk, Him stands nervously downstage left, and She is upstage center pantomiming the taking of notes.

UNIT III: A Doctor's Office.

She is the physician, Him is the patient, and He is the laboratory assistant. She stands upstage of the examination table, Him stands left of the desk, and He stands down rightstage holding a specimen jar.

UNIT IV: A Confessional.

He is the priest, She is a statue of the Virgin Mary, and Him is the penitent. He sits in a chair centerstage and speaks with an Irish or Italian accent, Him kneels at the side of the chair stage right, and She poses on the desk upstage left.

UNIT V: A Draft Center.

Him is the inductee, He is a Southern general, and She is offstage right. Him stands shaking down center, and He sits in a chair upstage left. Him addresses the general by speaking directly to the audience.

UNIT VI: A Clearing in the Park.

He is offstage left as the voice of God, She is a sweet young girl of sixteen, and Him is a young lover. Him and She stand down right holding hands and looking above the heads of the audience, smiling and giggling.

UNIT VII: A Battlefield.

Him and She are medics, and He is a wounded soldier who screams and then stumbles forward into their arms. They are all downstage center and face the audience throughout the episode.

UNIT VIII: A Business Office.

Him is now the gruff-voiced employer and She is an older gum-chewing secretary. He is now the brash, youthful salesman. Him sits in a chair with his feet upon the desk, She is upstage center pantomiming the taking of notes, and He enters to stand nervously downstage left.

UNIT IX: A Cemetery.

Him lies on the bench with his head facing centerstage, as the deceased. She is the mournful wife and sits in a chair facing the bench. He is a scheming friend and stands behind the chair with his hand gently resting on her shoulder.

UNIT X: Limbo.

They stand in a straight line near the downstage center playing area facing the audience. He is right, Him is center, and She is left. They speak to the audience as robots and as the characters indicated in the suggested stage directions. Him tries to cover his ears whenever he is not speaking.

UNIT I: A Living Room.

[1] Shakes her finger at Him.

[2] Throws up her hands in disgust.

[3] Shakes his finger at Him.

[4] Places her hand under Him's left shoulder.

[5] Places his hand under Him's right shoulder.

[6] They yank Him to his feet.

SHE: [1] Where have you been?

HIM: Wandering around.

SHE: Wandering around. [2] I don't know why you can't be a man; you just wait till the Army gets a-hold of you, young man.

HE: [3] They'll make a man of you—.

SHE: Straighten you out. [4]

HE: A little regimentation. [5]

SHE: Regulation. [6]

[7] Spinning Him around.

[8] Spinning Him around. On each of the short lines that follow, He and She take turns spinning Him from one of them to the other.

[9] Leans over and whispers in Him's ear.

[10] Straightens up and shouts in Him's ear.

[11] Shakes his finger at Him.

[12] Shakes her finger at Him.

[13] Glaring at Him.

[14] Glaring at Him.

[15] Meekly.

[16] Pulls his ear.

UNIT II: A Business Office.

[17] Nervously shifting weight from one leg to the other.

[18] Takes a deep breath.

[19] Leans forward.

[20] Turns to She and shakes his head.

[21] Turns back to Him.

[22] Shuffles feet.

[23] Rises indignantly.

UNIT III: A Doctor's Office.

[24] Moves to Him and begins the examination.

[25] Turns to He and winks.

[26] Turns to Him and winks.

UNIT IV: A Confessional.

[27] Whispers.

HE: Specification. [7]

SHE: Indoctrination. [8]

HE: Boredom.

SHE: You'll get up and go to bed.

HE: Drill; march.

SHE: Take orders.

HE: Fight.

SHE: Do what they tell you.

HE: Keep in step.

SHE: Do your part.

HE: Kill a man.

SHE: [9] You'll be a better person to live with, believe me. [10] As a matter of fact, your father and I are getting damned tired of having you around.

HE: Looking after you. [11]

SHE: Making your bed. [12]

HE: Keeping you out of trouble.

SHE: [13] How old are you, anyway?

HIM: Sixteen.

HE: Sixteen—well, my God. [14]

SHE: Shouldn't you be drafted before long?

HIM: Two years. [15]

SHE: You just better toe the mark. [16]

HE: How long at your present address?

HIM: Six months. [17]

HE: Any previous experience as an apprentice?

HIM: No, sir. [18]

HE: Where did you live before that? [19]

HIM: I was just wandering around.

HE: Not good. [20] Draft status? [21]

HIM: Well, [22] I haven't been called but—

HE: We like fighters on our team, fellow. [23]

HIM: Well, actually I'm a conscientious—

SHE: [24] Sit down. Roll up your sleeve. Take off your shirt. Stick out your tongue. Bend over, open your mouth, make a fist, read the top line. Cough. (HIM coughs.)

SHE: Very good. [25]

HIM: Thank you.

SHE: Perfect specimen. [26]

HIM: I do a considerable amount of walking.

HE: I don't follow you.

HIM: I don't believe in war. [27]

HE: There's no danger of war. Our country is never an aggressor.

28 Whispers.

29 Angrily rises.

30 Crosses himself and quickly rises.

UNIT V: A Draft Center.

31 Remains calm and polite throughout this episode.

32 "Service is compulsory" music may be played here.

33 Rises, steps from behind desk, and clicks his heels.

34 Salutes audience.

35 Salutes audience.

36 Salutes audience while Him shakes his head at the audience.

37 Turns and faces Him, smiling.

38 Moves behind the desk and sits, looking at papers.

39 Looks up, holding the signed papers.

40 Turns to He, takes a few awkward steps up stage center.

41 Prances about a few steps, and then rushes to the desk and kisses He on the cheek.

42 Smiles and then rises and points Him offstage left.

UNIT VI: A Clearing in the Park.

43 Moves center stage with hands extended.

44 Meets her center stage, and they walk hand in hand downstage center.

45 She sits on the ground.

46 Him kneels behind her and points to the stars just above the audience's head.

47 An eerie voice offstage right.

48 Another eerie voice offstage left.

HIM: But armies, see—I don't believe in it.

HE: Do you love your country? 28

HIM: No more than any other, the ones I've seen.

HE: That's treason. 29

HIM: I'm sorry. 30

HE: Quite all right; we'll take you.

HIM: I won't go. 31

HE: 32 Service is compulsory.

HIM: It's my right.

HE: You'll learn. 33

HIM: I don't believe in killing people.

HE: For freedom? 34

HIM: No.

HE: For love? 35

HIM: No.

HE: For money? 36

HIM: No.

HE: We'll teach you. 37

HIM: I know, but I won't.

HE: 38 You'll learn.

HIM: I can't.

HE: You're going.39

HIM: I'm not.

HE: You'll see.

HIM: I'm sure.

HE: You'll see.

HIM: I'm flat-footed.40

HE: You'll do.

HIM: I'm queer.41

HE: Get lost.42

SHE: I'm lost.43

HIM: I'm sorry.44

SHE: Aren't you lost?

HIM: I wasn't going anyplace in particular.

SHE: That's unnatural.

HIM: I was just wandering.

SHE: What will become of you?

HIM: I hadn't thought of it.

SHE: You don't believe in anything.45

HIM: But you see, I do.46

HE: I see.47

HIM: It's just that no one else seems to believe—not really.

HE: I see.48

[49] Another eerie voice offstage up center.

[50] Another eerie voice offstage down left.

[51] Sits next to her.

[52] Hugs him.

[53] Breaks away from her roughly.

[54] Rises angrily.

[55] Rises angrily.

[56] Slaps Him and walks off toward stage right.

[57] Faces audience, rubbing his face, and then moves down left.

UNIT VII: A Battlefield.

[58] He stumbles on stage from down left.

UNIT VIII: A Business Office.

[59] Pats He on arm and moves center with Him.

[60] Hanging up the imaginary phone.

[61] Holds out an imaginary phone.

[62] Crosses to Him and slaps him hard on the back.

[63] Coughs and collapses on desk.

[64] Raises head.

[65] Rises and moves to Him, stage left.

UNIT IX: A Cemetery.

[66] Pats her shoulder.

[67] Pats his hand.

[68] Whispers in her ear.

[69] Rises and faces He, smiling seductively.

[70] Puts her arms around He's neck.

[71] Kisses He passionately.

[72] Runs her hands through He's hair.

[73] Puts his arms around She's waist and starts to lead her downstage center.

UNIT X: Limbo.

[74] Voice of Mother.

HIM: Like this pride in country.

HE: I see.[49]

HIM: And this pride in blood.

HE: I see.[50]

HIM: [51] It just seems that pride is such a pointless thing; I can't believe in killing someone for it.

SHE: [52] Oh, my God, honey, it isn't killing; it's merely nudging out of the way.

HIM: But we don't need it.[53]

SHE: Think of our position, think of me, think of the children.

HIM: I am.[54]

SHE: [55] You're shiftless is what it is.

HIM: I'm really quite happy; I don't know why.

SHE: Well, how do you think I feel?[56]

HIM: Not too well, really.[57]

SHE: Where does it hurt?[58]

HE: Nothing to worry about.

SHE: Yes, sir.[59]

HIM: Thank you.[60]

SHE: And that's all for the morning; Mr. Trader is on line six.[61]

HIM: Thank you; send Wheeler in.

HE: How are you, old boy?[62]

HIM: Not well, [63] I'm afraid.

SHE: Don't be; it isn't serious.

HE: Just been working too hard.[64]

SHE: Why don't you lie down.[65]

HE: Best thing for you.

SHE: I know, but he was quite handsome—a gentle man.

HE: [66] Bit of a radical though—not good for the family.

SHE: I know.[67]

HE: You're better off.

SHE: I have a life of my own.

HE: . . . you have a life of your own.[68]

SHE: He was such a lost lamb.[69]

HE: Never agreed with anyone.

SHE: Arguments everywhere we went.[70]

HE: What kind of disposition is that?

SHE: I don't know what I ever saw in him.[71]

HE: You need someone who knows his way around.

SHE: I do.[72]

HE: I do.[73]

Pause.

SHE: [74] I don't know why you can't be a man.

[75] Voice of Father.

[76] Voice of Mother.

[77] Voice of Employer.

[78] Voice of Doctor.

[79] Voice of General.

[80] Voice of Sweet Young Girl.

[81] Voice of God.

[82] Voice of Sweet Young Girl.

[83] Voice of Scheming Friend.

[84] Voice of Mournful Wife.

[85] Voice of God.

[86] Faces audience, speaks in normal voice.

[87] Voice of Secretary.

[88] Voice of Him as the Boss.

[89] Voice of the Brash Salesman.

[90] Voice of Mournful Wife.

[91] Voice of Mother.

[92] Voice of Him as the youth in Unit I.

[93] Voice of the Father.

[94] Faces audience, speaks in normal voice.

[95] Voice of God.

[96] Faces audience, speaks in normal voice.

[97] Voice of the Secretary.

[98] Mournful Voice.

[99] Voice of Scheming Friend.

[100] Voice of Mournful Wife.

[101] Voice of Scheming Friend.

[102] Voice of Mother.

[103] Kneels, faces audience and pleads in a sad, mournful voice as the lights dim to a blackout.

HE: [75] Keep in step.

SHE: [76] Toe the mark.

HE: Draft status?[77]

SHE: Stick out your tongue.[78]

HE: You'll learn.[79]

SHE: What'll become of you?[80]

HE: I see.[81]

SHE: Think of the children.[82]

HE: Best thing for you.[83]

SHE: I do.[84]

　　Pause.

HE: I see.[85]

HIM: [86] I mean that can't be the way people want to spend their lives.

SHE: Trader on line six.[87]

HIM: Thank you.[88]

HE: Just been working too hard.[89]

SHE: I do.[90]

　　Pause.

SHE: Where?[91]

HIM: Wandering.[92]

HE: I see.[93]

HIM: [94] They'll believe anything anyone tells them.

HE: I see.[95]

HIM: [96] I mean that can't be the way people want to spend their lives.

SHE: That's all for the morning.[97]

HIM: Quite happy.[98]

HE: Best thing for you.[99]

SHE: I do.[100]

HE: I do.[101]

　　Pause.

SHE: Where have you been?[102]

　　Pause.

HIM: Can it?[103]

FROM

Lemonade (1969)
by JAMES PRIDEAUX

This avant garde play is fairly similar to the other plays in the series in its approach to the question of the meaning and purpose of life, but it is more provocative and stimulating because of its comic character types.

In particular, two matrons, Mabel and Edith, unexpectedly meet on a deserted highway in late afternoon to engage in a favorite occupation: selling lemonade. Although friendly and polite, the two women do not seem to be the best of saleswomen, and as a consequence they pass most of the time seeking to highlight their own personal accomplishments, even if it should mean an occasional exaggeration.

What emerges from their dialogue is the sad reality, however gleefully expressed at times, that loneliness and boredom are just as destructive and devastating as absurdity and that compassion and understanding may well be what give meaning to existence.

In playing the scene, the actors should be aware that even though the ladies are in their late fifties, they take a childish enjoyment in setting up the lemonade stand and preparing for business. There should also be an atmosphere of competition between the two, especially as they relate their stories and exaggerations. A good approach might be to imagine two little girls playing house but having difficulty deciding who will be the "adult."

Mabel, the slightly older matron, should be more timid and hesitant in her delivery and should wear a simple, but rather expensive, dress. Edith, more vocal and somewhat shrill, should be more forceful and self-assured. Both should wear large straw hats and carry enormous handbags, from which they might produce a variety of unusual hand props to help emphasize the absurdity of the situation.

Although the tone of the scene is for the most part laughable and foolish, there must be a concluding moment of poignancy and sympathy as the two ladies become more understanding and protective of each other's feelings.

Cast:
    Edith
    Mabel

Scene:
    A deserted highway at the edge of a small Midwestern town. Late afternoon.

ACT I

As the scene opens, Mabel enters hurriedly, carrying a large pitcher of lemonade in one hand and paper cups in the other. There is a smug air of wealth and sophistication about her manner that suggests elegance, and she takes care to arrange her paper cups in a neat and orderly fashion.

Just as Mabel has finished her arrangement, Edith enters carrying a large pitcher of lemonade, paper cups, napkins, toothpicks, and a sign that reads "Lemonade—2¢ a Glass." She stops abruptly upon seeing Mabel and drops everything except the lemonade.

The two ladies stand staring at each other for some time, their eyes moving from the

Lemonade

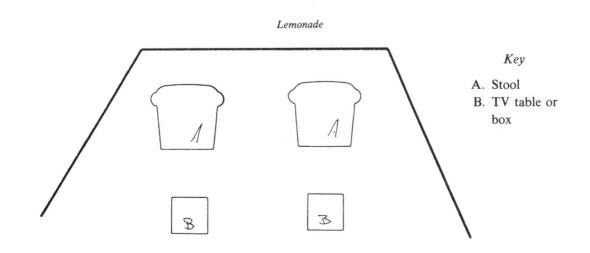

Key

A. Stool
B. TV table or box

pitchers to the lemonade stands, from the paper cups to the signs, and then from the napkins to the toothpicks, Finally, they begin to laugh in shrieks of joy and recognition.

<table>
<tr><td>

1. Mabel shrugs her shoulders.

2. Edith moves to her stand, and each audibly sighs as she pours a glass of lemonade.

3. Sits.

4. Moves to her stand and sits.

5. Takes a gulp of air and then speaks.

6. Choking on her own lemonade.

7. Sitting up as tall and erect as possible.

8. Puts cup down and glares at her.

9. Turns away.

10. Turns away.

11. Turns back to face Mabel.

12. Turns back to face Edith.

13. Rises and paces in a circle around her stand.

14. Back at her stool, she sits.

15. Sips from her cup.

16. Adjusts an earring.

17. Adjusts the other earring.

18. Arranges her hair.

19. Folds her hands in her lap.

20. Crushes her paper cup.

21. Removes a large paper bag from her purse and opens it with a flourish.

22. Placing the bag between them.

23. Drops her cup in the bag with a loud thud.

24. Halfheartedly gestures toward the audience.

25. Studies her cup before speaking.

</td><td>

EDITH: What are you doing out here in the middle of the highway selling lemonade?

MABEL: [1] I might ask you the same question. (They both take a sip of lemonade.) Now be honest, [2] Edith. Aren't you just as glad it's over?

EDITH: (With great seriousness.) Mabel, [3] I haven't told another soul this yet. But I want you to know.

MABEL: What, [4] Edith?

EDITH: I'm getting married.[5]

MABEL: You're what?[6]

EDITH: [7] I'm getting married.

MABEL: Edith, [8] you've *been* married for twenty-five years!

EDITH: I'm leaving Herbert and marrying somebody else.[9]

MABEL: [10] You can't be serious.

EDITH: I am.[11]

MABEL: It's unthinkable! [12] Why, you and Herbert *apart*. I couldn't imagine—

EDITH: [13] I've fallen deeply and desperately in love. This is the real thing at last, Mabel. It's the most beautiful thing that's ever come into my life and I don't intend to lose it.

MABEL: I can't *believe* it!

EDITH: [14] You probably think it's too late for me, but you're wrong. We're perfect together. He's a little older than I am, but I think that's all to the good. Mabel, we have such moments of . . . understanding. We read aloud to each other. We're halfway through "The Agony and the Ecstasy."

MABEL: Who is he?[15]

EDITH: He's a schoolteacher, [16] a widower. He's [17] not much to look at, [18] a little rough, a little homely, but very sensitive underneath. And he worships the ground I walk on.[19]

MABEL: Where does he teach?[20]

EDITH: (On guard.) What?

MABEL: [21] Where does he teach?

EDITH: (Hedging.) Where?

MABEL: Where?[22]

EDITH: [23] He teaches at the . . . Seqwaunie Junior High School. Out at the other end of town. He teaches music. Singing.

MABEL: [24] I never heard of it.

EDITH: It's at the other end of town.[25]

MABEL: (Holds up pitcher.) A little more lemonade, dear?

</td></tr>
</table>

26 Begins to whimper.

27 Rises and raises her voice dramatically. Then sits.

28 Begins to whimper.

29 Proudly displays her chin, leaning across her table to thrust it toward Mabel.

30 Rises and storms downstage left.

31 Turns and glares at Mabel.

32 Leans back and folds her arms across her chest.

33 Crosses back to her seat, sits, and pulls a comic book from her purse.

34 Turning the pages rapidly.

35 Reaches in her purse and pulls out an all-day sucker.

36 Rises quickly.

37 Licks the all-day sucker.

38 Offers Edith a lick of the all-day sucker. Edith makes a face and refuses.

39 Rolls up her comic book and points it angrily at Mabel.

40 Crosses her eyes to demonstrate.

41 Throws what remains of all-day sucker in her large brown bag.

42 Throws her comic book in the large brown bag and sits.

43 Nervously looks at her watch.

44 Leaning across her table.

EDITH: No, 26 thank you. (Mabel puts the pitcher down. They never drink again.)

MABEL: What about Herbert?

EDITH: Herbert doesn't need me.27

MABEL: Surely after twenty-five years, he—

EDITH: 28 Herbert Northrup has never *once* raised his hand to me. He's never cared enough even to *want* to. My friend at the Seqwaunie Junior High School once threw a copy of "Anthony Adverse" at me. (Proudly.) 29 I had to have three stitches.

MABEL: (Firmly.) Edith, *there is no Seqwaunie Junior High School.*

EDITH: (Rises.) 30 What did you say?

MABEL: I said there is no Seqwaunie Junior High School.

EDITH: Why . . . 31 you . . . *turncoat!*

MABEL: 32 I'm merely stating a *fact.*

EDITH: I don't want your facts! 33 You talk like some silly *man.* I *know* there isn't any Seqwaunie Junior High School. And for all I know there wasn't any Seqwaunie Hotel either, and I didn't sing, and Herbert wasn't sitting there. And I suppose I'm not a woman who watched her children go up in flames.34

MABEL: (Wearily.) 35 I really don't know.

EDITH: If it never happened, 36 why do I remember it so clearly? Why can I still smell the smoke?

MABEL: 37 Edith, lots of things that occupy our minds never happened and they never will. So there's no sense worrying about them. (EDITH sits, sullenly.) 38 I do admire you for decorating the children's graves, even if they're not dead. They will be one day and you'll be that much further ahead. As for this school teacher you've invented—

EDITH: 39 I don't care to discuss that. I might just mention that Marilyn isn't cross-eyed and Randolph is not a cripple, either.

MABEL: But I did *try.* I tried everything to get Marilyn's eyes to cross. I had her doing eye exercises in *reverse,* 40 reading small print in dim light—*everything.* And as for Randolph, 41 I was forever putting obstacles in his way, a box here, a bucket there. He was just too nimble for me. They were wonderful children. It was the least I could do for them. (There is a pause. Then EDITH speaks with great significance.)

EDITH: 42 Do you remember Miss Gundlach?

MABEL: Raymond's secretary? 43 Of course. A lovely woman.

EDITH: (Hitting every word.) 44 They copulated time and time again . . . over and over!

MABEL: (Rising, stunned.) That's . . . not . . . true!

EDITH: It was common knowledge. He kept a room above the

[45] Whispers softly.

[46] Throws her watch in the brown bag and sits.

[47] Begins to whimper as she slowly rises and moves stage right.

[48] Sighs very loudly.

[49] Moves swiftly to her stool and sits.

[50] Reaches into her handbag and pulls out a fan, which she strokes vigorously.

[51] Fans herself even faster.

[52] Rises, snatches Edith's fan, and drops it in the large brown bag. Then she moves in front to mark her sign.

[53] Mabel discards her black crayon in the brown bag when she returns to her seat, and Edith repeats on her return.

[54] With icy coldness.

[55] Glares at Mabel.

[56] Glares at Edith.

[57] With icy coldness.

[58] Places her hand over her heart.

[59] Turns away.

[60] Turns away.

Seqwaunie Casino at the other end of town. [45] They went there at lunchtime every Monday, Wednesday and Friday, and he—

MABEL: That's impossible! Raymond had no interest in that— [46] no *need!*

EDITH: Sometimes they'd go on Tuesdays and Thursdays, too.

MABEL: (Deeply hurt, moves a step to right, looks away.) Why should he do that? I was waiting . . . I was willing . . . I always did the best I could.[47]

EDITH: (Blithely.) I wouldn't worry about it. So many of the things that occupy our minds never happened . . . and never will.[48]

MABEL: (Facing her grandly, her full height.) You're a gossip, Edith. I must ask you to leave. Please peddle your lemonade somewhere else.[49]

EDITH: It's a public highway. [50] I have as much right here as you have.

MABEL: Please *go.*

EDITH: *Never.*[51]

MABEL: (Rummaging in her bag.) Very well. [52] But I shall see to it that you do no business whatsoever. (She pulls out a black crayon and marches around to her sign. She then crosses out the 2¢ and makes it 1¢. She gives Edith a superior smile and resumes her seat. Edith, disturbed, rises, goes front, and reads Mabel's sign. Then she gets her bag, produces a black crayon, crosses out the 2¢, and writes: FREE.)

EDITH: (Leaning on the box.) Nobody, [53] but nobody, undersells Edith Northrup. (She goes grandly back to her stool and sits.)

MABEL: (After a moment, facing front.) I've never liked you very much, [54] Edith.

EDITH: (Also facing front.) The feeling is mutual.[55]

MABEL: [56] I've always found you uninspired. Tawdry. Common.

EDITH: You're pompous. [57] Overbearing. Stupid.

MABEL: *Shallow.* (EDITH lets this go by for an instant, but only an instant.)

EDITH: For your information, I am a woman of . . . [58] unplumbed depths. All right, I admit it's too late, but I'm still . . . un-plumbed.

MABEL: [59] You make yourself sound like a bathroom fixture.

EDITH: You needn't sound so smug. [60] You're in the same boat. I'll tell you one thing. If I'd been Mrs. Raymond Lamston things would have been different.

MABEL: I suppose that would make me Mrs. Herbert Northrup.

EDITH: I wouldn't be surprised.

[61] Shaking her head in disbelief.

[62] Rises quickly.

[63] Sinks back down on her stool.

[64] Looking skyward, and then facing Mabel.

[65] Suspiciously.

[66] Turns away, afraid to face her.

[67] Clasps her hands over her ears, afraid of what Edith might say.

[68] Edith gently reaches over and removes Mabel's hands from her ears.

[69] Mabel searches desperately in her handbag for a tissue.

[70] Hugging her tightly for comfort.

[71] Wiping her eyes, and then straightening her dress.

[72] They both sigh in unison.

[73] Discards the handkerchief in the large brown bag.

[74] Adds the last line as an afterthought.

[75] Hands on hips, shaking head.

MABEL: Well, [61] I don't believe I'd care for that.

EDITH: Oh yes, [62] you would. Anyway, you don't know *what* you'd care for. Heaven knows, *I* don't. [63] Half the time I find I don't care for what I thought I cared for at all. It would have been nice, I admit, if I'd dropped a lit cigarette on the living room carpet and the children had gone up in flames. A lovely glow for a moment. But afterward they really would have been dead and I would have missed them. [64] They've kept me going for a long time. Do you know what I think our trouble is?

MABEL: Whose?[65]

EDITH: Ours. Everybody's. I think . . .

MABEL: [66] I'm not sure I want to hear.[67]

EDITH: I think the trouble is that way deep down we're filled with—

MABEL: If this is going to be unpleasant, I—[68]

EDITH: It's *love*, Mabel. I think that way down deep we're filled with *love*. I mean *way* deep down where you sometimes can't even see it, you don't even know it's there. Now *that* poses problems. Here we are on this planet, Earth, and— (But MABEL has made a choking sound and buried her face in her hands.) Why,[69] Mabel! (She rises, goes to her.) What is it?

MABEL: I'm sorry. I'm being such a fool. (EDITH produces a handkerchief from her pocket and gives it to MABEL)

EDITH: [70] You just go ahead and have a good cry. (She pats her.) Better now?

MABEL: Yes, thank you. I don't know what came over me. Out here on the highway, [71] too.

EDITH: What do you care what *they* think? All right.[72] (MABEL nods and EDITH goes back to her stool.)

MABEL: (Dabbing her eyes with handkerchief, speaking to herself, really.) I really am sorry. [73] This isn't like me at all. It was only . . . despair . . . that made me do it. All these years, and I've just never found the answer. At first I thought it was going to be . . . physical contact . . . but it wasn't. And then . . . human relationships . . . weren't to be counted on—they changed like the wind. And religion turned out to be . . . a bit of a fraud . . . all man-made. I don't know. I sometimes think . . . the best you can do . . . is just to be kind . . . to everybody . . . [74] and keep pets.

EDITH: (Lightly, sympathetically.) [75] Is *that* all you've been worried about?

MABEL: Isn't that enough?

[76] Very confidentially, in a hushed voice.

[77] Reaches into the brown paper bag and pulls out the handkerchief. She unfolds it, dabs a last tear, and then blows her nose rather noisily.

[78] They sigh audibly in unison.

[79] Places her lemonade pitcher on Mabel's stand.

[80] Begins to fold her tablecloth.

[81] Moves to Edith to help her fold the tablecloth and collect her glasses.

[82] They laugh for an uncomfortable moment, and then both sigh audibly in unison.

[83] Reaches into her handbag and pulls out a rose, which she gives to Mabel.

[84] Sits stirring the lemonade with one hand and holding the rose in the other hand as the lights fade.

EDITH: Well, [76] I'll tell you what you do. You simply go home and fuss with Raymond a bit and rustle up something good for dinner and watch a little television and go to bed.

MABEL: I won't be tired.[77]

EDITH: Well, read in bed for a while. Put some soft music on the radio and read in bed. How can life get better than that? [78] (She sighs, looks out toward highway.) I don't think I'm going to sell a thing. I might as well go home. (She rises, looks at MABEL.) You coming?

MABEL: Not just yet.

EDITH: I'll leave my things here. [79] Who knows, you may sell all of yours and mine, too. (She goes to MABEL, who rises, and they touch cheeks.) Goodby, my dear.

MABEL: Oh. (She returns the handkerchief, uses a social tone of voice.) Thank you. It's been *awfully* pleasant.

EDITH: (Crosses back of stools.) [80] You must come by for dinner one evening soon.

MABEL: (Cozily, also crossing back of stools.) [81] We'd love to. And you folks be sure and stop by whenever you're in the neighborhood. Raymond's always saying, "Let's have Edith and Herbert over."[82]

EDITH: (She starts to exit, turns, and coming back to MABEL, speaks with sudden fervor.) [83] I wish you'd been at the funeral. It was such a beautiful service. If I do say so, we did very well by the children. (She exits.)

MABEL: (Sits, looks out at the highway a moment, then calls timidly, sadly.) Lemonade! Lemonade! Get your lukewarm lemonade here![84]

FROM

The Runner Stumbles (1976)
by MILAN STITT

Although based upon an actual Michigan murder case of the early part of the twentieth century, this drama derives its sensitive but thought-provoking impact from the simplicity of the characters, the complexity of the situation, and the creativity of the staging.

Related primarily in a series of flashbacks, the plot concerns the trial of Father Rivard, an unconventional and somewhat abrasive priest who is charged with having killed a young nun, sister Rita. Although the priest denies any knowledge of the crime, there are grave doubts concerning his innocence.

The Runner Stumbles

As the play begins, Father Rivard is in prison awaiting trial. He is exhausted and confused, primarily because he cannot recall the circumstances that led to his imprisonment. As he is speaking with a court-appointed lawyer, there is an abrupt change in his attitude and mood; he suddenly begins to recall the past, including the isolated episodes involving Sister Rita.

In playing the scene, the actors are reminded that it is a recollection by the priest and should have a dreamlike quality in performance. If possible, lights should be dimmed to almost dark to suggest an atmosphere of gloom and despair, or soft music may be played in the background to initiate the audience into the flashback approach.

Although the scene concludes with rejection and a degree of physical violence, the opening exchanges of dialogue suggest a romantic attraction between Father Rivard and Sister Rita. Care should be taken to highlight the awkwardness and insecurity they feel in trying to express themselves, especially since they are alone in the nun's room.

The actors should strive for a realistic style of performance, even though the scene is a memory, and the tone of the dialogue should be both intimate and conversational. The argument that propels the climax of the scene should not be exaggerated or overly forceful, but should grow out of mutual misunderstanding of what has been said or implied. There should also be a sense of emptiness and frustration as the scene concludes and the characters are left alone with their own personal torment and sadness.

Cast:

> Nun
>
> Priest

Scene:

> The nun's room. It is late April, 1911.

ACT II

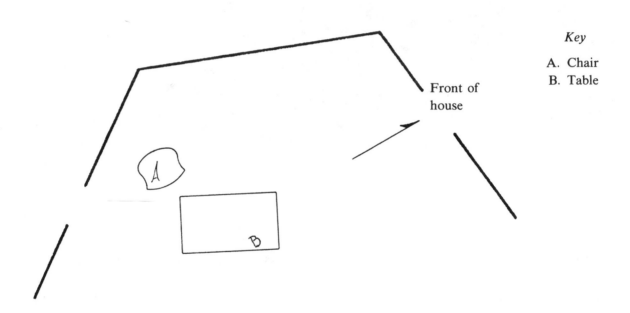

Key

A. Chair
B. Table

Front of house

As the scene opens, Sister Rita is staring blankly through an imaginary window facing the audience, sobbing. A fire has just swept through the rectory grounds, destroying her beloved rose garden, and she is clutching one of the remaining buds in her hand as Father Rivard enters.

The priest abruptly stops as he notices that Sister Rita is wearing street clothes, and he starts to retreat. She turns quickly and realizes that he is about to leave. There is a moment of innocent, childlike laughter as both try to conceal the awkwardness of the situation. As they relax and become more comfortable with each other, the conversation becomes intimate and flirtatious but builds to an unexpected climax.

As the scene opens, the Nun is down center, the Priest is offstage right, and Mrs. Shandig is offstage left.

[1] Clutches a small black book.

[2] Kneels stage right, facing center.

[3] Strokes her hair.

[4] Lifts her face toward himself.

[5] They hold hands.

[6] She crosses left of the table. He stands to follow her with his eyes. The table separates them.

[7] They sit down left.

[8] They are shoulder to shoulder.

[9] She gently rests her hand on his leg.

[10] Reaches for the diary.

[11] Their hands meet, and they pause.

[12] She takes the book and flips through the pages.

[13] She hands it to him.

[14] She gently touches his chin.

NUN: (At window.) [1] Where is my garden? The fire ditch. They dug the fire ditch right through my garden. All the bulbs are dug up. The roses. They burned. (During the NUN's speech, PRIEST abruptly enters, crosses to NUN. PRIEST holds NUN until sobbing subsides. NUN [2] falls to knees in front of PRIEST, who sits on stool.)

PRIEST: [3] At night I wonder how you are feeling, what you think, if you're happy, if you can sleep. Even when I pray, I wonder what you're doing. I look up through a window if it's recess or listen for your steps in the hall. [4] I can only concentrate if I pray about you. Almost to you. (He is about to kiss her.)

NUN: Please. Tell me what it is.

PRIEST: I have. (Silence.) I love you. (They kiss, stand and embrace.)

NUN: (Sitting on stool as PRIEST sits on bench.) [5] I never dared think—I thought who else would have me but the Church? But with you I'm not nothing, am I?

PRIEST: No. You're not.

NUN: (Standing to put diary away.) I'm just like everyone else.

PRIEST: What's that?

NUN: (Starting to pass PRIEST.) [6] Just my diary. I always keep it in the drawer. But it's all right now, isn't it? (Handing it to PRIEST.) Do you want to read it?

PRIEST: It's drawings.

NUN: Not all of it. (She sits on bench with PRIEST to look at diary.)[7]

PRIEST: No. [8] Of course not. This can't be Sister Immaculata, can it?

NUN: [9] I think she must have been in a grump that day.

PRIEST: Every day. Did you show her this?

NUN: [10] No one's ever seen it. I offered to show it to Mother Vincent, but she said the only sin it could possibly be is boring.[11]

PRIEST: She was wrong. This is so easy. Why was I so stupid? I don't understand why it seemed so worthy to—

NUN: Why do we have to understand? [12] Has trying to understand been so wonderful?

PRIEST: No.

NUN: Who's that?[13]

PRIEST: Me? Well, you sure got the eyelashes. How could you know how I'd look without a beard.

NUN: I guessed.[14]

PRIEST: Well, you'd be disappointed.

[15] He places his arms around her shoulders and cradles her.

[16] Leading him by the hand downstage center, facing the audience. During this exchange, she never takes her eyes from the town.

[17] They are arm in arm.

[18] He turns away from her.

[19] She continues to stare at the imaginary houses.

[20] He breaks away from her and moves several steps up center.

[21] She turns to face him and holds out her diary.

[22] He takes several more steps away from her, up center.

[23] She glances at the extended diary, confused.

[24] He moves to her, grabs the diary, and leads her to the chair.

[25] The Priest forces the Nun to sit, thrusts the diary before her face, and stands behind her, with his hands gripping the back of the chair.

[26] Deliberately placing his arms at his sides.

[27] Clasps the diary to her bosom.

[28] Crosses quickly down center, followed slowly by the Priest.

[29] Grabs the Nun by her hand and spins her around.

[30] He crosses quickly down right.

NUN: I don't think so.

PRIEST: [15] You make me so happy. And you made me so miserable.

NUN: I never meant to. [16] (Leading PRIEST to window, still holding diary.) Look. Where I stood all those nights. See. We can be with all the other people now. We aren't so different after all, are we? Don't look at the Church. Look down there with the other families. We'll be like that too.

PRIEST: [17] We can't move down there.

NUN: We'll have our own children.

PRIEST: [18] Children.

NUN: Oh yes. [19] I should have known. Oh, all those nights. Known that if the Church wasn't everything, that you would give me something in its place. I think I always knew I was not a true Bride of Christ.

PRIEST: You thought of this before.[20]

NUN: No. Just the confusion. [21] In there you'll see. I just didn't know.

PRIEST: [22] What did you write?

NUN: It doesn't matter, [23] does it?

PRIEST: Read it to me.

NUN: Someday, whenever, you can read it all—

PRIEST: Read it to me. [24] Now. Read it.

NUN: (Looking as she sits on stool.[25]) Well, any page these last few weeks. "I think Father Rivard must be right. Maybe the Church is only for rules, but God is for people. According to the rules everything I feel is wrong, yet nothing feels wrong. Do I have a conscience? Yes, I do. Do I belong in the Church? I don't know. He makes me so confused."

PRIEST: [26] We can never lose our faith.

NUN: We won't.[27]

PRIEST: You can't even think of it.

NUN: (Standing.) Now look. [28] The lights are going on in their homes. We can think of that. We'll be down there and then— (PRIEST suddenly pulls her from the window.) What is it?

PRIEST: [29] Mrs. Shandig is coming up the hill.

NUN: But we can tell her. Everyone.

PRIEST: No.

NUN: Why?

PRIEST: (Moving to exit.) Because I, [30] I—I'm their priest. She depends on me. They all do. I'm the only way they have of understanding.

NUN: People understand. (She crosses to stop his exit. He grabs her by the arms.)

³¹ Mrs. Shandig appears up left and moves in slow motion to up center, where she freezes.

³² Places diary on the table and moves quickly to him.

³³ Grabs him around the neck, pleading.

³⁴ Breaks away from her roughly, takes the chair and moves it beside the table downstage, where he sits and faces the audience. The Nun slowly advances toward him.

³⁵ She leans forward, trying to press her face to his.

³⁶ He jumps up and turns to her.

³⁷ He twists her neck viciously.

³⁸ Releases her and then reaches for the diary.

³⁹ She kneels on the floor and begins to gather up the torn pages. He hovers threateningly above her.

⁴⁰ He also kneels, and they face each other over the torn diary.

⁴¹ Rises and heads for down right.

⁴² Rises and follows to block the exit.

⁴³ He slaps her. Mrs. Shandig relaxes her freeze, takes several steps forward, and then kneels in prayer; crossing herself, she faces the audience.

PRIEST: ³¹ It's not how you think it is. Their homes have photographs of babies in coffins. Adolescents pour kerosene on kittens, and their fathers laugh when they set the fire. Sometimes wives cannot cook breakfast. Their fingers are broken from their husbands' beatings. It's only because they think I'm different; it's only because they think I'm worthy that I can help them. I must be worthy.

NUN: (Putting arms around his neck.) ³² I think you're worthy. Please. You said you loved me. I know you're too good, too precious to escape, ³³ desert me when—

PRIEST: I'm not, not what you think. I, I, I've destroyed all that. For the Church. (Pushing her onto stool.) ³⁴ There's nothing left for you. I can't be a husband. I can't be (Kneeling in front of her.) a father. There's nothing left but cruelty. That's all I know. That's all I worship. All I need. Not the resurrection, life. It's the nails. My salvation. Only the agony. There's no chance for—

NUN: You're not cruel. ³⁵ It'll be different now.

PRIEST: Damn you. ³⁶ Trying to break me down, make me forget. (Taking her head in his hands, forcing her to look out window.) ³⁷ Planting those flowers out there as if you, you could make the world beautiful. What makes you think you could change anything? Promising me things will be better. You make them worse. It's not my fault you lost your faith. ³⁸ It's not. You never had any if it dies so easily. (He starts to rip up diary. She wrestles it from him.)

NUN: No. ³⁹ That was before. You can stop. That's gone. It's gone.

PRIEST: (Grabbing NUN by shoulders, shaking her with violence, causing her to drop diary.) With them, with them, ⁴⁰ I can make it look all right. They only want me to say those words. They don't want to know me. You can't know me. I'll destroy you. You can't know me. You'd hate me. I hate myself.

NUN: I don't hate you. God doesn't hate you.

PRIEST: (Trying to exit.) ⁴¹ Don't talk about God.

NUN: (Holding him from exit.) ⁴² We still have God.

PRIEST: I don't want God. ⁴³ I don't want you. (Starting to choke NUN.) I hate God. I hate God. I want to kill God. I always wanted to kill—. (NUN falls to floor. For a moment of silence, she appears dead. PRIEST slaps her on back. She coughs. He drags her to bench. He gets wet cloth, sits next to her, wiping her brow. MRS. SHANDIG begins to enter up ramp. She is looking back down in the valley to see if fire is out.)

44 Holding her hand to her throat.

45 He cradles her in his arms as Mrs. Shandig rises from prayer and enters up left.

46 Mrs. Shandig halts abruptly when she enters and sees the Priest and the Nun in this intimate embrace.

47 The Nun turns to face Mrs. Shandig, as the Priest retreats several steps downstage right.

48 Moves slowly to the Nun.

49 Turns to Priest, who turns away.

50 Kneels to comfort the Nun.

51 Screams out loud and buries her head on Mrs. Shandig's shoulder.

52 Rises quickly and slowly backs away toward the stool.

53 Crosses above the table and heads for the exit, up left.

54 Rises and rushes after him.

55 Turns quickly and holds the Nun from him at arm's length.

56 Rises and takes several steps toward him.

57 Raises a menacing fist as she moves to pull the Nun from the Priest's neck.

58 Pulls the Nun and Mrs. Shandig apart, and then leads the Nun to the bench. Mrs. Shandig retreats slowly up center, and does not lower her fist throughout the scene.

59 They sit, and the Priest puts his arm around the Nun's shoulders.

60 The Nun rests her head on his shoulder.

61 The Priest rests his head on her shoulder.

62 Whispers to him.

63 The Priest rises and pulls the Nun to him in a tender embrace.

64 The Priest slowly retreats toward up left in a trancelike state, with his arms extended toward the Nun.

65 The Nun halts, then rushes upstage left. She stops short of where the Priest exited and collapses in a fit of tears as the lights slowly fade.

NUN: (As she stops choking.) I'm sorry. 44 I'm sorry. What you said. Hating God. It's my fault too. You couldn't—

PRIEST: No. No. It's me. (MRS. SHANDIG enters.)45

NUN: We have to help each other. It's all we have now. We only have each other. (PRIEST crosses right as he sees MRS. SHANDIG.)46

MRS. SHANDIG: (moving to hold NUN.) Sister. What are you saying?

NUN: Please. 47 Mrs. Shandig. Leave us alone.

MRS. SHANDIG: What is wrong? 48 What you said . . . (NUN throws herself into MRS. SHANDIG's arms for comfort.)

NUN: Tell her. 49 Please tell her.

MRS. SHANDIG: Tell me what?50

NUN: Tell her.51

MRS. SHANDIG: Tell me what?

NUN: (Turning from embrace to PRIEST.) Just tell her, and it will be over. Please. Tell her you love me. (Silence as MRS. SHANDIG goes, sits on stool.)

MRS. SHANDIG: Sister. 52 No. No.

PRIEST: 53 There'll be a train. I'll walk to Traverse City. The fire didn't affect the trains there.

NUN: I'll go with you.54

PRIEST: No.55

MRS. SHANDIG: Father, 56 you can't go.

NUN: (Suddenly embracing PRIEST.) Don't leave me. I don't care if I go to hell.

MRS. SHANDIG: (Pulling NUN from PRIEST.) Father, 57 you hear her. (About to hit NUN.) Don't touch him.

PRIEST: (Catching MRS. SHANDIG's hand.) Stop it. 58 (NUN crosses to PRIEST. Both sit on bench.) I won't hurt you anymore. You can leave. But you must leave the right way, when your community tells you. Go back to your order.

NUN: I'm not a nun now. 59 I'm nothing.

PRIEST: 60 There's still a place for you. They need you.61

NUN: I haven't even said it to you.62

PRIEST: Don't say anything. Don't think it. Honor your vows. It's the only way. (MRS. SHANDIG backs, unnoticed by audience, to witness chair, where she sits at end of scene.) 63 The rest is me. I cause it. God isn't cruel.

NUN: (Crying, hitting PRIEST.) No. No. No. There's nothing left. (As PRIEST crosses to cell and sits on stool.) 64 But I never told you. You never heard the words. Let me tell you.65

EPILOGUE

Following are some suggested readings that the beginning actor may wish to acquaint himself with as he continues to explore meaningful scene study and play interpretation. A practical application of the theories and exercises in these texts should provide a solid foundation for approaching more difficult and complex scenes in future performances, and should also reveal the extraordinary possibilities available to the beginning actor as he seeks to realize his own creative performance potential.

Benedetti, Robert L. *The Actor at Work.* Englewood Cliffs, New Jersey: Prentice-Hall, 1976.

Boleslavsky, Richard. *Acting: The First Six Lessons.* New York: Theatre Arts Books, 1933.

Cole, Toby, and Chinoy, Helen Krich. *Actors on Acting.* New York: Crown, 1970.

Dezseran, Louis John. *The Student Actor's Handbook.* Palo Alto, California: Mayfield, 1975.

McGaw, Charles. *Acting Is Believing.* Third Edition. San Francisco, California: Rinehart Press, 1975.

Kahan, Stanley. *Introduction to Acting.* New York: Harcourt, Brace and World, 1962.

Linklatter, Kristin. *Freeing the Natural Voice.* New York: DBS Publications, 1976.

Penrod, James. *Movement for the Performing Artist.* Palo Alto, California; Mayfield, 1974.

Spolin, Viola. *Improvisation for the Theatre.* Evanston, Illinois: Northwestern University Press, 1963.